# What the
# SCRIPTURES
## Teach Us about
# Raising
# a Child

# What the
# SCRIPTURES
## Teach Us about
# Raising
# a Child

## S. MICHAEL WILCOX

DESERET
BOOK

SALT LAKE CITY, UTAH

**Library of Congress Cataloging-in-Publication Data**

Wilcox, S. Michael.
  What the scriptures teach us about raising a child / S. Michael Wilcox.
    p. cm.
  Includes bibliographical references and index.
  ISBN 978-1-60641-130-8 (hardbound : alk. paper)
 1. Child rearing—Religious aspects—The Church of Jesus Christ of Latter-day Saints.  2. Child rearing—Religious aspects—Mormon Church. 3. The Church of Jesus Christ of Latter-day Saints—Doctrines.  4. Mormon Church—Doctrines.  I. Title.
  BX8643.C56W55 2009
  248.8'45—dc22                                         2009009632

Printed in the United States of America
Worzalla Publishing Co., Stevens Point, WI

10   9   8   7   6   5   4   3   2   1

I have no greater joy than to hear that
my children walk in truth.
*3 John 1:4*

# Contents

# CONTENTS

But now, O Lord, thou art our father;
we are the clay, and thou our potter; and we all are
the work of thy hand.
*Isaiah 64:8*

# Preface

The challenge in writing a book of this nature is dealing with one's own imperfections regarding the subject. I certainly have not mastered the delicate art of raising children myself, and at least part of the reason for authoring a book on this theme is to firm up in my own mind—in a manner only the discipline of writing can—all the lessons the Lord has shown me in the scriptures through thirty-five years of being a father. The opportunity to feel somewhat hypocritical has been present with me on practically every page. "Physician, heal thyself!" (Luke 4:23) has a certain validity here, and I have repeated it to myself frequently.

Yet I have profited a great deal in my attempts to raise our children by constantly referring to the mothers and fathers of sacred scripture for inspiration, warning, comfort, and counsel. They have seldom failed to provide ample material to ponder. I believe deeply in the principles taught by the Lord in the standard works about raising children. I accept them without reservation, insofar as I can discover them, but my own attempts to live them all in a way that satisfies my own level of expectation generally falls short. I assume that in these feelings we all sail in the same sea.

I have no desire to create guilt in the heart of any father or mother. We deal with enough parental unease as it is. My sincere hope and sole purpose is to present principles and ideas to peruse, ponder, and apply as appropriate to each family's individual situation. I can say without hesitation that among all the books and articles I have read over the years about raising a child, none has proved as valuable as the scriptures. They carry an authority and a convincing spirit even the most skilled and learned advisors do not. They provide examples and plainspoken admonition. They hold within their pages the wisdom of six thousand years and, therefore, are to a great degree immune from the trends and societal experimentation of a changing world. It is surprising how much one can find within their pages when we approach them with the single objective in mind of raising children.

I am sure what I have found useful to me as a father is not all-inclusive. The scriptures are inexhaustible, and no one has mastered them except the Master himself, though he has promised he will guide the least of us through them if we ask. May these thoughts generate an interest and a curiosity in you to search the Lord's word for encouragement and revelation to bless you in your parenting, the most intensely critical—and magnificently fulfilling—of all vocations. May you have the comfort—as you experience all the frustrations, apprehensions, and anxieties, as well as the elations, delights, and joys of being a mother or father—that the Savior himself lovingly spoke of your calling:

"And he took a child, and set him in the midst of them: and

when he had taken him in his arms, he said unto them, Whosoever shall receive one of such children in my name, receiveth me: and whosoever shall receive me, receiveth not me, but him that sent me" (Mark 9:36–37).

Having a child in our home may be the closest thing to having the Father and Son themselves within our walls.

Even so it is not the will of your Father which is in
heaven, that one of these little ones should perish.
*Matthew 18:14*

And he did exhort them then with all
the feeling of a tender parent.
*1 Nephi 8:37*

# Introduction

From the heights of Mount Sinai, Jehovah gave Moses the parameters of a peaceful and stable society in ten concise commandments. Among them we read: "Honour thy father and thy mother" (Exodus 20:12). From the very beginning, God knew there was great safety in placing a child under the sheltering guidance of parents. The fifth commandment is the Lord's validation of his confidence in the protective love and self-sacrifice of fathers and mothers. Honor is such a well-chosen word, for it carries so many connotations with it, including respect, obey, trust, revere, bring glory to, and act with integrity. All these terms fit the parent-child relationship. Yet it is the last half of the commandment that causes me to pause and reflect: "That thy days may be long upon the land which the Lord thy God giveth thee" (Exodus 20:12). As Paul tells us, this "is the first commandment with promise" (Ephesians 6:2).

What exactly does that promise assure? I long thought it had to do with an extended life and was individual in nature, but it doesn't take a very robust mind to realize that many do not honor their parents and yet live long, and many do honor their parents but die young. No, I think the promise has to do with the broader society and its ability to endure. We have seen decline and decay in countless civilizations that, in time, removed themselves from the land through self-destructive practices. What brings staying power? How can nations grow, flourish, and remain?

I believe the answer lies in that brief promise sounded through the thunder of Sinai. In the family! In the mutual respect and love of mother and father, parent and child! The child who learns courtesy, consideration, respect, civility, selflessness, control, and industry in a home will take those qualities into his or her wider world. Our culture will survive only if the roots of permanent and lasting human relationships are fostered, nurtured, and refined in the homes of its people.

When a child learns the fundamental lessons of human interdependence in the family, he or she will know how to transfer those lessons to a more extensive milieu. Here is the hope and the help so many search for but fail to find. If we would bless and heal our society, our gaze need reach no farther than our own walls. What kind of people will we send into the broader world from the moral schoolhouse of our homes?

Many centuries before Christ was born in Judea, the greatest of all Chinese philosophers, Confucius, established his nation's foundation upon this bedrock truth: "The gentleman devotes his efforts to the roots, for once the roots are established, the Way will grow therefrom. Being good as a son and obedient as a young man is, perhaps, the root of a man's character."[1] It is the great opportunity of mothers and fathers to help plant those roots and thereby bestow upon their world their most enduring and precious gift—a noble child.

In the restored gospel we know the consequences of our roles as fathers and mothers have an end as wide as eternity. How can our limited reach grasp that everlasting perspective and bring it to fulfillment? How do we help God make gods out of infants?

⌒

## CHAPTER ONE

Abraham received promises concerning his seed,
and of the fruit of his loins . . . out of the world they
should continue as innumerable as the stars. . . .
This promise is yours also. . . . Go ye, therefore,
and do the works of Abraham.
*Doctrine and Covenants 132:30–32*

# The Divine Apprenticeship

## UNDER THE MICROSCOPE

When I was young, I was fascinated with all that surrounded me. The world of nature presented before my wondering eyes the infinite marvel of God's creative genius. My mother fostered this interest and one day presented me with a used microscope she had obtained from a neighbor who taught high school biology. This was not a toy microscope but a genuine instrument of scientific technology set to amaze the eyes of a child.

I felt very adult and had an awe bordering on reverence as I switched the lower lenses and adjusted the mirror to send a shaft of light directly up to the eyepiece. This was joy indeed. Here was a new world to explore, and I went at it to the point of eyestrain. Peering into the tiny eyepiece became an obsession, especially when I examined living things. The first time I looked at a drop of pond water and saw dozens of varied miniscule creatures swimming across my field of vision was an intense interaction with life.

One day a new thought came to me. What would it feel like to be under the microscope instead of above it, with someone watching with equally keen interest my every move as I was watching the feverish life in the drop of water? The question came and went, and I never entertained it again—until I became a parent.

I had been taught that life was a test, a proving ground for immortality, an opportunity to win celestial glory. This, I felt, naturally meant an observing God watching my progress, my moral and spiritual development. However, I shall never forget the feeling of intense scrutiny that fixed on me the moment I held my first infant child. The question I had entertained as a boy suddenly became deeply relevant. I knew what it felt like to be under the microscope, with my Father in Heaven at the eyepiece. It was not an oppressive sensation. I did not feel like God was spying on me; rather I felt an intensity of loving interest which seemed to say, "This is very, very, very important!" His was an encouraging eye, full of affection and concern, similar to my mother's watching me from the sidelines of a game, cheering me on, eager for my success. But I have been vastly aware, from that moment on, that what I had engaged in by bringing this tiny human being into the world was crucial in a way which nothing I had done before could compare with.

I have often pondered why this is so. Why should I feel God's gaze in such a fixed way in my role as a father? Why was it so decisively vital that I learn how to do this right? To this day I continue to feel the Lord's intense interest—his penetrating concentration. It is not critical, nor judgmental, nor condemnatory, but I have never doubted his desire that I learn the essential lessons of parenting and make them an integral part of my being, as second nature as breathing.

Surely it has to do with the development of another divine soul—that of my child—but there is more. The answer lies in every prayer we utter. Since my earliest recollection I have addressed God as "Father," the heavenly parent. With the birth of my first child, mortality became an apprenticeship for Godhood.

## "ENTHRONED IN GLORY"

We do not use formal apprenticeships much anymore, but in the past they were the way to teach young people a trade. Learners were allowed to do, on a smaller scale and under a master's tutelage, what they would one day do on their own and in a larger arena. It is a foundation principle of the Restoration that the purpose of life is to learn to become like our Father in Heaven. Godhood is parenthood of a grand magnitude, but before we can progress to that degree of glory, we are given the opportunity to learn here on earth the essential principles of parenthood. We can refine within the sacred boundaries of the family in a tiny dimension what God does, and what we are destined to do, on a galactic, cosmic level. President Brigham Young once told the Saints that they were organized and designed and capacitated "to be enthroned in glory, to be made angels, Gods—beings who will hold control over the elements, and have power by their word to command the creation and redemption of worlds. . . . This is what you and I are created for."[1]

When we feel the joys, the quiet satisfactions, or the pleasing compensations of a father or of a mother, we enter in a minute degree into the mind and heart of God. When we experience the pains, the disappointments, and the sometimes crushing sorrows of those same roles, we also comprehend the soul of Deity. There is no school for developing character nor for attaining the attributes and perfections of godliness like raising a child. There is no accomplishment which will require greater dedication, intellect, and the refined emotions of the soul than to raise a child to dignity, independence, and holiness in a decadent and fallen world. Yet the rewards are incomparable and offered both in an earthly and an eternal dimension. Can we, as does our Father in Heaven, exalt and lift another soul to a higher level? If we learn to do so here, during our mortal apprenticeship, the eternal possibilities become infinite. Little wonder that we feel the close scrutiny of the Lord's watchful gaze with its intensity of hope and anticipation. He would share with us, his children, the qualities, the everlasting joys, the incomparable fulfillments of his own "work and glory."

## THE DIVINE MANUAL

In light of these overwhelming possibilities, both for ourselves and our children, it would not be surprising to believe, even to expect, that the Eternal Father would have some counsel to offer us regarding our roles as fathers and mothers. I am sure that most parents are aware of many other publications offering sound ideas, practical experience, and scholarly advice about rearing children. These all can be profitable to us, but we would be less than astute if we did not also seek to use the Lord's manual, his handbook, for he is the Father of fathers, and no amount of earthly understanding can equal what he could suggest to anxious parents desiring to be wise.

Where is the apprentice's manual, the hands-on, do-it-yourself instructions? As in so many varied areas of life, the scriptures are sufficient for our needs, and we can discover rather quickly how much counsel they offer when we read them searchingly with a parent's mind. With godly perception the Lord has inspired the writers and compilers of sacred writ to include within those pages stories, examples, and instructions necessary to give us direction. With that focus comes a calming influence the scriptures uniquely supply to enable us, under the direction of the Holy Spirit, to apply those lessons to our own families with their varied challenges and personalities. It is to the scriptures we can—and should—turn in this most critical of mortal apprenticeships.

## CHAPTER TWO

And God blessed them,
and God said unto them, Be fruitful, and multiply,
and replenish the earth.
*Genesis 1:28*

# Genesis—First Families, First Lessons

## JOY AND REJOICING

It becomes apparent with even a cursory reading of the first book of the Old Testament, Genesis, that it is a book dealing exclusively with families. Almost without exception, every story in Genesis involves family relationships. It is as if the Lord said, "Because the family is so important in your godly apprenticeship, I will focus on it before any other truth, challenge, doctrine, or virtue." Its lessons are beautiful in their simplicity. Here are a few of them: Adam and Eve—stay together, and don't eat forbidden fruit! Isaac and Rebekah, Jacob and Rachel—a righteous, covenant wife is without price and worth every effort to obtain. Jacob and Esau, Joseph and his brothers—if someone hurts you, forgive them, especially if they are members of your family. Eve, Sarah, Hagar, Rebekah, Leah and Rachel, and even Tamar—children are desirable, a cause of rejoicing, a blessing from the Lord. Interwoven throughout Genesis—indeed, throughout the Old Testament—is this yearning desire for offspring. It is the first great message the scriptures impart about children.

Joy and rejoicing in posterity is included in the Lord's instructions to Adam and Eve in the Garden of Eden. "And God *blessed* them, and God said unto them, Be fruitful, and multiply, and replenish the earth" (Genesis 1:28; emphasis added). Notice that this injunction is placed in the frame of a blessing rather than as a direct commandment. It is repeated in the most sacred environs of the temple. Though they left the Garden of Eden for a number of reasons, surely having children was a prime one.

Eve later commented on that decision: "Were it not for our transgression we never should have had seed" (Moses 5:11). Lehi added his witness to this truth about the Fall in his final words to his son Jacob: "And they would have had no children" (2 Nephi 2:23). Eve's very name breathes with the dignity of motherhood: "And Adam called his wife's name Eve, because she was the mother of all living" (Moses 4:26). This is enhanced by understanding how in ancient societies a name was closely linked to the vital essence of an individual. To give a name to something was almost akin to creating it, to state its intrinsic, inborn nature, to identify the most defining quality inherent in it.

After the story of Adam and Eve in the Old Testament we rapidly move through the Flood to the story of Abraham and Sarah. The first thing we learn of Sarah is that "she had no child" (Genesis 11:30). The central theme of their lives is the promise of children, a posterity as numerous as the sands of the sea and the stars of heaven. Every detail we know of them revolves around this focal point. After decades of patient but painful waiting, the long sought for blessing is announced first to Abraham and then to Sarah.

"Then Abraham fell upon his face, and laughed" (Genesis 17:17). The same Hebrew word is used in describing Sarah's reaction. "Sarah laughed within herself, saying, After I am waxed old shall I have pleasure . . . ?" (Genesis 18:12).

We may misunderstand the word "laughed" in these two verses. The word in Hebrew can equally be translated "rejoiced." In truth, Joseph Smith changed *laughed* to *rejoiced* when describing Abraham's response to God's announcement (JST Genesis 17:23). This was not disbelieving, mocking laughter, but a rejoicing, too-good-to-be-true, celebratory laughter. Later, when Isaac was born, he was given the name "laughter," for Isaac means "to rejoice." The joy of having children was so overwhelming that Sarah believed anyone who heard her story would understand and share her happiness: "And Sarah said, God hath made me to laugh, so that all that hear will laugh with me" (Genesis 21:6). This is joy that is manifested not only in the mind, in the heart, in the soul but also physically, in the outward expression of warm, delighted laughter.

Rachel's desire for children is as poignant as any in sacred writ. After watching her sister, Leah, give birth to four sons in succession, she cried out to her husband, Jacob, "Give me children, or else I die" (Genesis 30:1). When she finally gave birth to Joseph, she named him with the hope, almost assurance, that "the Lord shall add to me another son" (Genesis 30:24). Among all the trials life dealt to Jacob, it was his perceived loss of children that brought from him the most agonized cries: "Me have ye bereaved of my children: Joseph is not, and Simeon is not, and ye will take Benjamin away" (Genesis 42:36). Later, as Judah pleaded for Benjamin when Joseph's cup was found in his sack of corn, he told Joseph that Jacob's life was "bound up in the lad's life" (Genesis 44:30).

The healing, redemptive, liberating joy of begetting children is expressed by Joseph at the birth of his two sons, Manasseh and Ephraim. In Joseph's mind they more than made up for more than a decade of slavery and unjust imprisonment, and this joy was articulated in the meaning of the boys' names: Manasseh means "forgetting" and Ephraim means "fruitful."[1] At their birth, he proclaimed this compensatory joy: "And Joseph called the name of the firstborn Manasseh: For God, said he, hath made me forget all my toil, and all my father's house. And the name of the second called he Ephraim: For God hath caused me to be fruitful in the land of my affliction" (Genesis 41:51-52).

We cannot separate the idea of family from Genesis, and the thread that binds so many of the stories together is the happiness of having children. That lesson is one the Lord wished to impress upon our minds from the very beginning—in the first book of the Bible. In a world of declining birthrates, neglected children, abortion, and abuse; in a world where children are sometimes seen as a burden, a hindrance to adult fulfillment, it is a message we need to hear again and again.

## "CHILDREN ARE AN HERITAGE OF THE LORD"

This theme of elation, of joy and rejoicing in children, is stressed repeatedly in stories throughout the Bible. The Hebrew midwives who refused to kill the Israelite baby boys were rewarded with posterity. "Therefore God dealt well with the midwives. . . . And it came to pass, because the midwives feared God, that he made them houses" (Exodus 1:20-21)—"houses" in this case meaning descendants.

Two of the most compassionate and selfless women of the Bible, Ruth and Naomi, were likewise blessed. Boaz told Ruth, "The Lord recompense thy work, and a full reward be given thee of the Lord God of Israel, under whose wings thou art come to trust" (Ruth 2:12). Under those loving wings the compensation chosen by God was posterity. "The Lord gave her conception, and she bare a son." This child would be to Ruth, and to Naomi in particular, "a restorer of thy life, and a nourisher of thine old age. . . . And Naomi took the child, and laid it in her bosom, and became nurse unto it" (Ruth 4:13, 15–16).

When Hannah gave birth to Samuel she expressed her gratitude in a triumphal hymn of praise: "My heart rejoiceth in the Lord. . . . There is none holy as the Lord: for there is none beside thee: neither is there any rock like our God" (1 Samuel 2:1–2). After consecrating Samuel to the Lord's service, she was blessed with more children. "The Lord visited Hannah, so that she conceived, and bare three sons and two daughters" (1 Samuel 2:21).

For the solicitous kindness she showed Elisha, the Shunammite woman (who was barren) was told, "About this season, according to the time of life, thou shalt *embrace* a son" (2 Kings 4:16; emphasis added). The choice of verb in this passage is particularly appropriate.

Gabriel's message to Zacharias in the temple announcing the birth of John was done in a tone of celebratory delight. "Thy prayer is heard; and thy wife Elisabeth shall bear thee a son. . . . And thou shalt have joy and gladness" (Luke 1:13–14). Did not the Psalmist understand this soul-stirring pleasure in children when he wrote centuries earlier, "Lo, children are an heritage of the Lord: and the fruit of the womb his reward. As arrows are in the hand of a mighty man; so are children of the youth. Happy is the man that hath his quiver full of them" (Psalm 127:3–5).

~

## CHAPTER THREE

Train up a child in the way he should go: and when
he is old, he will not depart from it.
*Proverbs 22:6*

# How Shall We Order the Child?

## MANOAH'S QUESTIONS

Continuing our study of what the scriptures teach us about raising children—that we might receive the promised joy they bring—let's look at Judges 13. Here we learn of two questions asked by the apprehensive parents of Samson before he was born. An angel appeared to Samson's mother to announce that she would bear a son. He would have special abilities and callings which would be used to free his people from the domination of the Philistines. He was to be a "Nazarite," an individual specifically dedicated to the Lord's purposes. Just so, our own children have special abilities and callings which will be used in their life's journey. There are things they will do and challenges they will face. We can anticipate definitive counsel from the Lord for each child.

Samson's mother was given precise instructions about what she was to do during her pregnancy. Herein is a fruitful thought. Before the child was ever born, she herself was to be clean. Her own life, in anticipation of that of her child, was to be dedicated to God, in whose service her son would be enlisted. "Behold, thou shalt conceive, and bear a son," the angel told her, "and now drink no wine nor strong drink, neither eat any unclean thing" (Judges 13:7). Crucial preparation in rearing a child begins in the lives of the parents, in the choices they make often years before their children are conceived.

When told by his wife of the angel's declaration, Manoah, Samson's father, "intreated the Lord, and said, O my Lord, let the man of God which thou didst send come again unto us, and teach us what we shall do unto the child that shall be born." When his request was granted, Manoah asked, "How shall we order the child, and how shall we do unto him?" (Judges 13:8, 12). When I read this story as a young father, it was very comforting to realize that the God who was sending these young spirits to my wife and me was willing to "teach us what we shall do unto the child that shall be born." That education would be exact and detailed regarding each individual child. Yet I sensed I needed to ask specific questions and devote time to pondering the answers he might give in relation to each particular child. God did send the angel back to Manoah and his wife, and instruction was given in response to their very important questions.

I do not think when I knew my first child was to be born that I realized how much the Lord wanted to instruct me concerning my children. I certainly pondered my coming role with a new anxiety but not with any awareness of a source of help to which I could turn. In his kindness to my wife, me, and our newborn child, the Lord provided a marvelous and totally unexpected tutorial. In the hospital, the first time I took my daughter into my arms, I could hear the voice of our Father in Heaven speaking to me through the thinness of the veil that is so immediate at the birth of a baby. He was telling me things about this specific child, just as he told Samson's mother. They were positive things, character traits she possessed, truths that we could share with her later in life when those endearing words from her Eternal Father would mean so very much. He also gave us direction concerning her specific gifts, how we could amplify them, warnings we would need to give heed to as she grew. It was tender advice given from one Father to a new father and a new mother as the transfer of a beloved child took place.

A few years later, when her sister was born, I wondered if the same experience would be forthcoming. I did not yet dare to ask for it, but as my second daughter was laid in my arms I tried to wait expectantly, to show the Lord that I was willing to receive his counsel if he were pleased to offer it. I was not disappointed, as once again those soothing feelings settled over our family in the hospital room and the guidance came.

I have to admit that, in spite of the powerful way the still, small voice spoke on these occasions, I sometimes doubted the reality of the counsel. Yet as our daughters grew through infancy into childhood, it became deeply apparent that the qualities the Lord had shared with us were dominant characteristics in our children. Others would notice and comment on those very gifts which our daughters displayed. When our sons were born, I was ready not only to silently wait for the Spirit to instruct me but to invite it. I cannot relate powerfully enough how wonderful those revelatory moments were and how profoundly they touched me. Five times the experience came, with each child a different explanation, with specific gifts, attributes, and directions, always positive, always lifting. Our children are adults now, and there is no longer doubt in my mind that the qualities pronounced at their birth are key elements in their personalities. We may go to the Lord, asking him to "teach us what we shall do" with each child, for each one is distinct and singular, and each one is his child too.

I am impressed that Manoah and Samson's mother were eager to ponder how they would raise their unique child even before his birth. We may handicap ourselves as parents to a great degree if we wait to ask those critical questions until our children reach their late childhood or teenage years. Although we will be asking follow-up questions with each succeeding stage of a child's maturity, there is weight and confidence in considering what God wants us to know before the actual responsibilities of parenthood descend on us.

It is hard when we are young to think about parenting and how our present actions might help or hinder our future effectiveness, but these are questions that must be addressed if we wish to avoid perplexing dilemmas later. It is also hard to contemplate deeply and seriously the qualities we will need as father or mother when first married and facing the pressures of a new, deeply committed relationship, schooling, employment, home purchase, and other responsibilities. Yet it is desirable that discussions between a husband and wife relating to "order[ing] the child" be done early. I have sometimes asked my college-aged single students who are dating what activities they are doing or discussions they are having which may give them ideas about the parenting desires or skills of their prospective spouses. That is vital knowledge. When our children are older and we are pressed by busy work and Church schedules, it becomes increasingly challenging to take time for serious contemplation and conversations, but Manoah's questions must be asked consistently and pondered often.

I have wondered in reading the story of the birth of John the Baptist about Elisabeth's self-imposed seclusion immediately after the conception of her son. Luke 1:24 tells us that "Elisabeth conceived, and hid herself five months." I suppose she spent long periods seriously thinking about how this child would be ordered. Perhaps those five months were set aside by Elisabeth for that very purpose. Now, my child—or yours—may not be, like John or Samson, foreordained to play out his or her divine commission on the world stage of scripture; however, in my heart and in yours, is he or she not worthy of equal consideration and deep moments of reflection?

Pondering the ordering of a child, as Manoah and his wife did, gives us the great opportunity to begin training a child very early in life; it gives us, as well as our child, a heading to sail towards. It enables us to emulate the counsel Alma the Younger gave to his son Helaman—"O, remember, my son, and learn wisdom in thy youth; yea, learn in thy youth to keep the commandments of God" (Alma 37:35). In large measure whether children can receive that wisdom depends on the earliest direction given to them. Alma also spoke to his son Shiblon of the formation of an initial habit of goodness: "As you have commenced in your youth to look to the Lord your God, even so I hope that you will continue in keeping his commandments" (Alma 38:2).

## NAAMAN'S QUESTION

Another question worthy of examination as we contemplate our roles as parents is one we would do well to consider in the initial stages of our children's lives. It was asked by Naaman, the Syrian leper who went to Elisha to be healed. Elisha did not come out to meet him, nor did he offer Naaman healing in the manner the leper had anticipated. Elisha simply told him, "Go and wash in Jordan seven times, and . . . thou shalt be clean. But Naaman was wroth, and went away, and said, . . . Are not Abana and Pharpar, rivers of Damascus, better than all the waters of Israel? may I not wash in them, and be clean?" (2 Kings 5:10–12).

Fortunately for him, Naaman had wise servants, who told him, "If the prophet had bid thee do some great thing, wouldest thou not have done it? how much rather then, when he saith to thee, Wash, and be clean?" (2 Kings 5:13). Naaman humbled himself, went to the Jordan, washed seven times, and the promised healing was granted.

There is a great lesson in this story. Far too often we want to do things our way instead of the Lord's way. Occasionally we may feel we are the exception or think we have a better idea than the counsel of the prophet. Scripturally speaking, we may be tempted to wash in the rivers of Damascus instead of the Jordan. That is surprisingly true and, when rearing children, far too frequently our first impulse.

When I was a new father, beginning the family journey with only my firstborn, I conversed with my mother about my new responsibility. My mother is a woman of great faith, and I have learned to trust her insights, so I asked her Manoah's questions in my own manner: "How do you raise righteous children?" I felt I could ask her this question because she had been fairly successful with her own children. She was a single mother, because my parents had divorced when their children were quite young. It was her sole influence that skillfully carved our characters. My sisters and I are not great bastions of goodness, but we followed and are still following the straight and narrow path to the best of our ability.

At the time I asked my mother that question, there had been no serious problems in our lives, and the future looked bright then and continues so to this day. I anticipated a deep answer of insightful complexity, so I was surprised by the simplicity of what she told me. With a certain ironic smile she said, "Well, Mike, your mother was too stupid [her word exactly] to think she had a better program than the Lord's. So I just did everything the Church told me to do."

That one statement reveals much about how we children were raised. She washed in the Jordan—not the rivers of Damascus—and the desired promise was delivered. I know this pattern will not always produce the results we desire. Sometimes in spite of all our truest efforts, our children exercise their agency, and disappointment, even tragedy, can result. But our best opportunity for success lies in washing in the Jordan, in doing it the Lord's way.

That way usually does not require great deeds. Naaman anticipated and was willing to accomplish "some great thing." But his servants suggested "how much rather, then" do the simple thing that had been asked (2 Kings 5:13). That is the Lord's way. It is sometimes surprising to see the lengths to which parents will go and the sacrifices they will make for children in sports or music or some other equally worthy activity, all of which are wonderful and good, but there may be equally great if not greater power in molding a child's heart and mind in the tiny daily acts suggested by the Lord. It is not in the great deeds but in the accumulation of repeated simple acts wherein rest the sweetest blessings.

Remember, Naaman had to bathe seven times in the river. Why seven times? Why not only once? How many home evening lessons do we teach before the gospel sinks into a child's heart? How many family prayers? How many vacations do we share, how many moments in quiet conversation before love is solidified? How often do we search a scripture narrative? How frequently do we bear testimony, or visit the temple, or sing in church, or walk in nature, or help with an assignment, or read a story, or relate a tale from our own lives before the rod of character grows strong in a child's soul? These are all simple things, but when repeated over time, with love, the blessing descends and joy results.

CHAPTER FOUR

*And the child grew, and waxed
strong in spirit, filled with wisdom: and the
grace of God was upon him.*
*Luke 2:40*

# The Lens of a Mother's Soul

## "MY SOUL DOTH MAGNIFY THE LORD"

One of the most remarkable parents we read about in the scriptures is Mary. What a tremendous responsibility was laid upon this young mother—that of nurturing the Savior of the world during his early years and young manhood. As we read the few accounts of Jesus' relationship with his mother, there is no question that mutual trust and reverence flowed between mother and son. Jesus' willingness to do what his mother desired him to do at the marriage at Cana and her returning confidence in him is a prime example. That willingness carried on throughout his life, and in his final moments on the cross, the bond between them was demonstrated by the Savior's concern for her future welfare as he commissioned his beloved disciple John to care for her.

When Jesus was found teaching in the temple at the age of twelve, Mary's mildly chiding question, his seemingly enigmatical reply, which she did not fully understand, gives added insight (see Luke 2:43–50). This was no power struggle by either of them, yet even at this early moment in his development, when the dawning realization of his life's mission was settling upon him, "he went down with them, and came to Nazareth, and was subject unto them: but his mother kept all these sayings in her heart" (Luke 2:51).

There will be in our lives moments when our children say or do things under the guiding influence of the Father, things which we do not understand. These will be moments to ponder, to keep in the heart, as Mary did at this time, as she had earlier after the visit of the shepherds (see Luke 2:19). In time, awareness will come as we gratefully realize forces are at work in the lives of our offspring to shape them and prepare them beyond the scope of our own efforts. We are not alone in our responsibility to create the foundations upon which they will build their lives. There is such comfort in that thought.

Yet of all the things we know of Mary, the woman whose name is so closely associated with that of "mother," it is her words to Elisabeth which have given me much insight into the role of parents, especially that of mothers. After Elisabeth's greeting, which recognized Mary as "the mother of my Lord," Mary responded, "My soul doth magnify the Lord, and my spirit hath rejoiced in God my Saviour" (Luke 1:43, 46–47).

When we magnify something, we enlarge it to fill our field of vision. Think of a magnifying class for close-up work, or a pair of binoculars or a telescope for things far in the distance. Small things are made larger, prominent, given a totality of focus. If we think of the many areas of life to which we might turn our prioritizing lenses, it is helpful to ponder that it was toward the spiritual, toward her God, that Mary pointed her soul. Hers was not a magnification that grew out of duty but a magnification she rejoiced in. There was no sense of obligation or hesitancy but only a free, joyful acceptance of God's will.

With this in mind we can muse on the profound effect this joyful attitude might have had on her son. A mother's soul is a lens through which a child almost always first sees God. Of course, we cannot be sure, but it is not a stretch to think of some profound conversations between Mary and Jesus regarding her sacred memories of the Annunciation, the overshadowing by "the power of the Highest" (Luke 1:35), the birth, and the visit of the Magi. Who first revealed to Jesus the meaning of all these things and the reality of his Father if not Mary? She filled his vision with her God and his God, her Father and his Father. Jesus was raised by a mother who felt a deep, rejoicing reverence for God. His own magnification and rejoicing in his Father is surely at least a partial reflection of his mother's own attitude just as his words in Gethsemane, "Nevertheless not my will, but thine, be done" (Luke 22:42), reflect those of Mary, who earlier had said, "Behold the handmaid of the Lord; be it unto me according to thy word" (Luke 1:38).

## HEAVENLY FATHER'S LITTLE CREATURES

What is the relevance of all this for you and me? We are invited to take a similar magnifying and rejoicing position. In my own life, it was my mother who enlarged God in my eyes—brought him up close so he filled the field of my vision. I saw him first through the lens of her faith, her soul, and it filled me with wonder and awe.

I said before that I was born loving all living creatures. It is important for children to learn how to love. Love is such a central, key virtue to instill in the heart of a child, and animals are a natural avenue to that final goal, for children gravitate to them instinctively and warmly. I had almost every species and variety of pet a little boy could have, from hamsters to canaries, and numerous dogs. In addition, I loved to roam the fields, ponds, and hills near my home in California to catch anything I could lay my hands on. I brought home in triumph (to eagerly show my mother) a vast assortment of lizards, horned toads, frogs, snakes, salamanders, insects, rabbits, and birds. Instead of recoiling in fear or disgust at the newest member of my growing menagerie, she would bend down to my level, look intently at the snake dangling from my hands, and say, "Which of Heavenly Father's little creatures did you bring home today, son?"

I learned to love God because I first loved his creations, his "little creatures," but it was my mother who focused that gaze heavenward. I believed my Heavenly Father created horned toads for little boys to catch. I still believe that. What other real purpose could they possibly have?

My family used to go to the beach, where I would roam through the tide pools and catch sand crabs as they washed in with the waves. They would tickle the palms of my hands, which for a small boy was an intense delight. I grew up believing God made sand crabs to tickle children's hands. I still do! As I grew, my mother took my sisters and me to the national parks in the western United States where, once again, the majesty of God was pointed out, this time on a more regal scale.

The stories of the scriptures were unveiled in like manner as we learned of God's graciousness to people of the past. I can still hear my mother's voice reading to me the stories of the Bible and the Book of Mormon and commenting on their lessons. There was eagerness and fervor in her voice. I knew she loved the stories she related and believed in them. Nephi wrote, "My soul delighteth in the scriptures, and my heart pondereth them, and writeth them for the learning and the profit of my children. Behold, my soul delighteth in the things of the Lord" (2 Nephi 4:15–16).

A child can sense the delight in the tone of a parent's voice, in the energy with which a mother tells a scripture story or a father speaks of the things of God. Delight is such a motivating emotion. It is the polish that brings clarity to the lens of the soul. Those things we delight in will naturally reflect upon our children. My mother filled my vision with God, and through the magnification of her soul I could see that he was wondrous, kind, and good. He was a being to rejoice in, to delight in!

I can think of no finer example of God's using the soul of a parent, a mother in particular, to instill faith in a child than the following story published a number of years ago in the *Ensign*. It is from the journal of a seventh-grade young woman named Stephanie:

> One day while we were reading our scriptures, we talked about how important it is for each of us to have our own knowledge and testimony—and that we must not put off asking Heavenly Father for this. That night I went to my room and shut the door. I waited until everything was very quiet. Then I knelt down by my bed and prayed. I asked Heavenly Father to please send me an angel to tell me for sure if the gospel was true. He answered that he would, and I was to get in bed and wait for the angel to come. I felt very peaceful and happy, and I waited.
>
> The house was very still, and I think I had dropped off to sleep. I woke up when I heard a voice. It was Mother. She was kneeling beside my bed

praying. She was praying for me. I listened, and when she finished I touched her hair so she would know I was awake. She put her arms around me and held me and her face was wet. She told me I had a Father in Heaven and that he loved me. She said she was glad he had let me come to live in our family. She told me he sent his own Son here to give his life so we could return to live with him if we obeyed his commandments. She told me to always remember that the gospel had been restored, and I must live it so I could go back to my Father.

We held each other for a while . . . and then Mother left. After she left, Father in Heaven said to my mind, "I sent you your angel."[1]

## CHAPTER FIVE

And they shall also teach their
children to pray, and to walk uprightly
before the Lord.
*Doctrine and Covenants 68:28*

# Stir Up Their Faith to Feel After God

## FEEL AFTER GOD

I have imagined having a conversation with the Father or the Son in which I was invited to ask them a question. Which question of the many that have passed through my mind down the years would I choose? I think it would be this one: "How do you instill faith in the heart of a child?" I should like to hear their answer as it relates to my roles both as a father and a grandfather and also as a teacher of youth for more than thirty-five years. Other questions are equally valuable, but that is the one I would select. Perhaps I would word it this way: "I have five children and five grandchildren. What do you want me to do for them that will be most important in securing for them a happy life and a joyous eternity? And could you make it simple? Just a few wise all-encompassing words to distill the essence of truth?"

I believe I have received an answer to that question. I found it in *Lectures on Faith*. The second lecture gives a fairly detailed description of the great patriarchal line stretching from Adam to Abraham. Among these great spiritual men, faith was passed down through the generations, parent to child. One afternoon I read these words:

> From this we can see that the whole human family in the early age of their existence . . . had this knowledge [a knowledge of God] disseminated among them; so that the existence of God became an object of faith in the early age of the world. And the evidences which these men had of the existence of a God, was the testimony of their fathers in the first instance.
>
> The reason why we have been thus particular on this part of our subject, is that this class may see by what means it was that God became an object of faith among men after the fall; and *what it was that stirred up the faith of multitudes to feel after him*—to search after a knowledge of his character, perfections and attributes, until they became extensively acquainted with him, and not only commune with him and behold his glory, but be partakers of his power and stand in his presence.[1]

The words "stirred up the faith" fairly leaped from the page, and I could feel the Spirit press their import into my mind. "As a father, you must stir up the faith of your children to feel after God." That was my commission as simply as the Lord could put it. That stirring up of faith did not end when they were teenagers or when they left home or when they were themselves married and then parents of children. It was not complete until they knew their Father in Heaven "extensively," could "commune with him," "behold his glory," and "stand in his presence." That is a lifelong pursuit and, depending on the maturity and disposition of the child, is achieved in stages.

That realization came in an overwhelming moment for me as a parent. Like the hub of a wagon wheel, I could fit all the spokes of parental skills into its central strength. Yet the very realization of this vital objective raised that most fundamental question: How? How do you stir up the faith of your child to feel after God?

Again the answer came in the second lecture of the *Lectures on Faith*.

## "GLORIOUS DISCOVERIES AND ETERNAL CERTAINTY"

We have now clearly set forth how it is, and how it was, that God became an object of faith for rational beings; and also, upon what foundation the testimony was based which excited the inquiry and diligent search of the ancient saints to seek after and obtain a knowledge of the glory of God; and we have seen *that it was human testimony, and human testimony only, that excited this inquiry*, in the first instance, in their minds. *It was the credence they gave to the testimony of their fathers, this testimony having aroused their minds* to inquire after the knowledge of God; the inquiry frequently terminated, indeed always terminated when rightly pursued, in the most glorious discoveries and eternal certainty.[2]

This is what I desire for my children: "glorious discoveries and eternal certainty." In the repeated emphasis on "human testimony" I had found my answer. To paraphrase the words of the Prophet Joseph Smith, human testimony excites and arouses inquiry and searching. These words perfectly match stirring up faith and feeling after God. In short, the testimony of a parent is a powerful tool for stirring up the minds of children to feel after God. Next to life itself, testimony is the greatest gift parents can give to a child—the sharing of their own faith, beliefs, and confirmations in such a way as to arouse in the mind of the child a desire to receive a testimony in like manner.

The truth of this idea is easily verified by a quick search through the Book of Mormon. Notice how many examples there are of a parent stirring up the faith of children to feel after God. Upon hearing Lehi relate his dream of the tree of life, Nephi writes, "After I, Nephi, having heard all the words of my father, concerning the things which he saw in a vision . . . , was desirous also that I might see, and hear, and know of these things, by the power of the Holy Ghost, which is the gift of God unto all those who diligently seek him" (1 Nephi 10:17). When the Spirit asked Nephi, "What desirest thou?" he replied, "I desire to behold the things which my father saw" (1 Nephi 11:2–3). Nephi's great visionary experience then followed. Lehi stirred up the faith of his son to feel after God.

While hunting beasts in the forest, Enos tells us, "the words which I had often heard my father speak concerning eternal life, and the joy of the saints, sunk deep into my heart. And my soul hungered; and I kneeled down before my Maker, and I cried unto him in mighty prayer" (Enos 1:3–4). The Lord responded to Enos's hunger, and he, too, received precious communication from heaven. Jacob stirred up the faith of Enos to feel after God.

While enduring the harrowing memories of his past life, Alma the Younger recalled a singular truth he had been taught about Christ. "I remembered also to have heard my father prophesy unto the people concerning the coming of one Jesus Christ, a Son of God, to atone for the sins of the world. Now, as my mind caught hold upon this thought, I cried within my heart: O Jesus, thou Son of God, have mercy on me" (Alma 36:17-18). Alma received the atoning mercy of the Savior, which changed his life forever. Alma the Elder stirred up the faith of his son to feel after God in the essential crisis of his youth.

Though these examples center on a father's influence, a mother's is equally powerful. One of the most endearing examples of a mother's influence is that of the mothers of the stripling warriors. As they prepared to go into battle for the first time, in response to Helaman's concern for their safety, they replied with a faith aroused and excited by the testimony of their mothers. "They had been taught by their mothers, that if they did not doubt, God would deliver them. And they rehearsed unto me the words of their mothers, saying: We do not doubt *our mothers knew it*" (Alma 56:47-48; emphasis added).

Notice that the specific wording is "our mothers *knew* it," not "our mothers *taught* it." These young men knew what their mothers knew, their own faith was aroused, and they were able to stand firm even when others gave way.

These are only a few examples. We could mention the influence of Mormon on Moroni, as evidenced in the letters he preserved, or that of Benjamin on his three sons, or the faith of Alma the Younger, which he passed down to his three sons. Some of these examples we will examine later. It is sufficient for now to see the power of a parent's testimony in exciting children's search for a knowledge of God and an ability to commune with him and eventually stand in his presence.

## ALMA'S TESTIMONY TO HIS SONS

In the Book of Mormon some of the richest veins to mine for counsel about raising a child are chapters 36 through 42 in Alma, which contain the final words of Alma the Younger to his sons. If we examine them carefully, we will see that they contain the essential parental quality of testimony.

Notice all the testimony words and phrases, for example, in Alma's advice to Helaman in chapter 36. He begins with, "*I swear unto you,* that inasmuch as ye shall keep the commandments of God ye shall prosper in the land"; "Learn of me; for *I do know* that whosoever shall put their trust in God shall be supported. . . . I would not that ye think that *I know of myself*—not of the temporal but of the spiritual. . . . God has . . . *made these things known unto me*"; "*I do know;* and the knowledge which I have is of God"; "*I know* that he will raise me up at the last day"; "Behold, my son, . . . ye ought *to know as I do know*" (vv. 1, 3–5, 26, 28, 30; emphasis added).

In Alma's words to his son we discover the full and personal account of Alma's three days of harrowing agony, which ended in his discovery of the Savior's mercy. This is one of the most beloved stories in the Book of Mormon, and it was related as a father's testimony to his son. We get a shorter version of it a few chapters later in Alma's words to his son Shiblon where, once again, we hear testimony words: "Now, my son, I would not that ye should think that *I know* these things of myself, but it is the Spirit of God which is in me which *maketh these things known unto me*" (Alma 38:6; emphasis added).

## FAMILY SCRIPTURE

I wonder how many times these young men had heard their father relate these experiences. Can you imagine them sitting there with a bored expression or saying to their father, "We know all this already, Dad. We've heard you tell it a million times."

The conversion of Alma the Younger was an experience we might term "family scripture." That it also became universal scripture is to our enrichment. Each family has such things. They are composed of the dreams, trials, conversions, and inspiration that come into individual lives. They are particularly useful in stirring up faith.

In my own experience, I recall my mother often telling us children what we termed "The Black Dog Story." It consisted of a remarkable answer to a prayer she offered as a young girl. On her walk home from school, the road climbed a hill and passed a house that had a huge black dog which sat on the front porch. If she and her brother started to run at the right time, they could get past the house and through a fence to safety before the dog could attack.

One day, however, she was alone and did not time her run correctly. The dog attacked, and she froze on the road. At the very moment the dog was leaping upon her she cried out loud, "Heavenly Father! Help me!" I can to this day still hear the tone of her voice and the change that came over it when she related this part of the story. She told us it was as if a hand reached down, caught the dog under the chin, and hurled him backwards. He then ran back to the porch, and she slipped through the fence and went home.

I never tired of hearing this story, nor do I cease to ask her to tell it to my children. It is family scripture, and it arouses feelings in my heart towards God every time I hear it. Written records of our ancestors many generations back can also have this effect. Perhaps that is one of the reasons we should write our life histories, especially those moments which have the potential to stir up the faith of future generations to feel after their Father in Heaven.

Is that not essentially what the scriptures are? Is that not one of the most motivating forces in turning the hearts of the children to their fathers?

## "YEA, I BELIEVE"

Before leaving the hub of parental responsibility to look at other things we might learn from Alma's words to his sons, we might ponder Alma 45. Alma's final counsel to his sons ends in chapter 42, but Alma does not leave the scene until chapter 45, which contains one last interview he has with Helaman. Here Alma asks his son some questions regarding his faith:

> Alma came unto his son Helaman and said unto him: Believest thou the words which I spake unto thee concerning those records which have been kept?
>
> And Helaman said unto him: Yea, I believe.
>
> And Alma said again: Believest thou in Jesus Christ, who shall come?
>
> And he said: Yea, I believe all the words which thou hast spoken.
>
> And Alma said unto him again: Will ye keep my commandments?
>
> And he said: Yea, I will keep thy commandments with all my heart.
>
> Then Alma said unto him: blessed art thou; and the Lord shall prosper thee in this land. (Alma 45:2–8)

I have thought about this exchange between father and son. We could use this as an example of several ideas, but I should like to focus on just one. Alma was providing an opportunity for his son to express his own testimony. A certain spiritual vigor accompanies the repetition of those simple words, "Yea, I believe." I have seen it verified, in both my own life and those of others, that when we share our testimony, when we express it openly, either vocally or in writing, it increases.

Water bags made from animal skin, the kind used in the ancient Near East, stretch when filled with liquid. When emptied and filled again, they can hold more as they continue to stretch. A testimony does likewise!

As we bear testimony, the Spirit refills it, but the soul's capacity to hold just a little bit more is increased. As life unfolds, the continual emptying and refilling of the soul enlarges its spiritual capacity and solidifies faith. It is therefore desirable to provide in positive, comfortable settings the opportunity for children to express what they believe, just as Alma gave that opportunity to Helaman with some simple questions immediately before "he departed out of the land. . . . and . . . was never heard of more" (Alma 45:18). We are given the opportunity of seeing Alma the Younger in many roles from rebellious youth to chief judge, to general, and to head of the Church, but it is as a father that he exits the stage of Book of Mormon narrative. Even in this there is a subtle, deeper-veined message.

A personal perspective might illustrate how important I feel this last point to be. I was born with a believing heart but a questioning mind. Through various periods of my life I have dealt with some doubts or questions that if I had given them room to grow, could have eaten away at my faith and become destructive of my testimony. Doubts sometimes feel like black holes sucking all the light out of me. I have dealt with college students who entertained some of the same uncertainties and have had conversations with numerous Church members struggling with similar issues. Rarely have I listened to someone besieged by an attack on their beliefs without being acquainted with the same onslaught in my own mind at some time in the past.

Doubt need not be destructive; it depends on how we deal with it. George MacDonald, a nineteenth-century minister, an author, and one of my spiritual mentors, once said, "With all sorts of doubt I am familiar. . . . Doubt is the hammer that breaks the windows clouded with human fancies, and lets in the pure light."[3]

I have many times imagined a conversation between me and the Lord wherein I explain to him my fear that my questioning mind will overcome my believing heart and I will fail in the great proving ground of mortality. Perhaps such an exchange took place before I was ever born. He always answers me in a way similar to this: "I will allow you to teach the gospel as your life's work. Every time you stand before a class or a congregation and begin to teach the realities of eternity, you will know that they are true, for I will fill you with a knowing mind. Just stand up and begin to speak!"

Sometimes I start a class or a talk feeling my soul is as empty as a dry lake bed and I have nothing to offer, but when I rise and begin to speak, the water of truth seeps in and fills me, and I know that I know. I am strengthened by my own voice. The memory of hearing the water flowing into me stays and sustains me even in the driest periods. I cannot emphasize enough how necessary it is for a parent to testify but also to help a child testify, to empty out what he or she believes, because the emptying provides enlarged room for the refilling.

～

## CHAPTER SIX

I call to remembrance the unfeigned faith
that is in thee, which dwelt first in thy grandmother
Lois, and thy mother Eunice; and I am
persuaded that in thee also.
*2 Timothy 1:5*

# The Footsteps of Fathers and Mothers

## EVERY ONE SEPARATELY

Alma's final words to his sons are introduced by a significant verse in the last section of Alma 35. The environment of their world is described, and it is not difficult to see the relevance of their world to ours. We are seeking to raise children of righteousness in a similar setting. We read: "The hearts of the people began to wax hard, and that they began to be offended because of the strictness of the word" (v. 15). More and more our stand on issues, principles, values, or what we consider appropriate behavior is being challenged. It was in the context of that world that Alma gathered his children "that he might give unto them every one his charge, *separately,* concerning the things pertaining unto righteousness" (v. 16; emphasis added).

This was not a formal family gathering but private, personal, one-on-one instruction. There is power in that type of individual attention to each child with his or her specific strengths, challenges, and maturity. The one-on-one times with our children may be the most effective moments we share. Sometimes they come as a gift, unplanned; other times we must seek to create such moments.

Our family likes to backpack. One of my daughters hikes slowly, while the rest of the family moves down the trail with considerable speed. I used to be somewhat annoyed that I would have to stay behind occasionally to walk with my daughter, encouraging her to pick up the pace to arrive at camp before dark. I soon learned what a gift was being offered me as we engaged in conversations surrounded by the beauties of nature. Somehow being away from distractions provided the perfect timing for some deep sharing. I soon learned to look forward to those calming, slow-paced walks. To this day the habit of walking with my daughter continues. She is the only child who always answers yes when I ask, "Who wants to go on a walk?" They continue to be some of my best moments with her.

With my other children, such moments come according to their interests and schedules. My wife and I have learned to create those times, often deliberately, and sometimes without being too obvious.

Each of our three sons was involved in Scouting, but their ages were spread far enough apart that we could not work on advancement with any two boys at the same time. We believed in Scouting, so we volunteered as counselors for every merit badge for which we could qualify—my wife for skills in art and music, and I for outdoor or nature badges. I used to wish the boys were closer in age so I would only need to do Reptile or Bird Study once, but I soon learned how wonderful those hours were, spent scanning the sky with binoculars for any new bird species we could find or catching insects to feed a hungry lizard. I believe the Scouting program sup-ported by the Church is valuable not as much for the skills or morals it instills in boys—which it does so well—but even more for the opportunity it gives parents for valuable one-on-one time with a son, if we are wise enough to take advantage of it.

Because of the edifying effects of these moments, we still try to encourage them, but they're on a more adult level now. My wife spends hours on projects with our daughters, and we have been able to take each child on overseas trips to learn about other cultures and religions. General family teaching and sharing are wonderful and necessary, and there is nothing like bringing the children and grandchildren together for mildly chaotic dinner or camping gath-erings, but few things can compare with giving "everyone his charge separately" (Alma 35:16).

## "ONE BY ONE"

Jesus demonstrated this imperative when he asked the parents gathered at Bountiful to bring their little children to him. After they were all placed upon the ground around him, he prayed for them as a group. We are told that the things he said could not be written, either because they were so profoundly beautiful or because they ex-pressed such eloquent truths. When he was finished, the children did not return to their parents. Rather, Jesus wept with joy, and "he took their little children, *one by one,* and blessed them, and prayed unto the Father for them" (3 Nephi 17:21; emphasis added).

It was not sufficient for the loving heart of our Lord to pray only for the multitude nor expressly for the children—no, Jesus deemed it necessary to bless and pray for each individual child. We know there were twenty-five hundred people in the gathering at Bountiful (see 3 Nephi 17:25). We do not know how many children were in that number, but even if the little children represented only one percent of the total, only twenty-five children, his blessing of each one would be a forceful lesson on the need to attend to our children also "one by one" (3 Nephi 17:21).

The Lord blessed me with an experience a number of years ago which increased my desire to share with my children on an individual basis. In Doctrine and Covenants 124 the Lord describes a way in which he often teaches us. Speaking to one of the early Church leaders, the Lord promises "he shall mount up in the imagination of his thoughts as upon eagles' wings" (v. 99).

The human imagination is a great conduit for the Holy Spirit to impart knowledge. From time to time the Lord lifts us up in the imagination of our thoughts and shows us wonderful truths. I call these experiences in my life "ponderings," for they often come while contemplating some truth of existence or of the gospel. On one such time I was pondering the Judgment.

Into my mind came an image of a waiting room, much like the waiting room in a doctor's office. The walls were lined with about twenty chairs, in each of which sat a man waiting to be called through a side door. To my surprise, when I looked closely at the men in the chairs, each one was me. There were about twenty Michael Wilcoxes waiting there.

In a short time, the door to an inner room was opened. I knew the Lord was on the other side and that I was going to enter into his presence for judgment. An angel came through the door, pointed at the man in the first chair, and said, "Would Michael Wilcox, the husband of Laura Wilcox, please come forward and render an account of his stewardship?" I watched as the first man rose, followed the angel, and closed the door. He was in the other room a long time and did not return to the waiting room.

In time, the door opened again, and the same angelic reception-tionist entered. He pointed to the man in the second chair and said, "Would Michael Wilcox, the father of Kirsten Wilcox, please come forward and render an account of his stewardship?" The man in the second chair rose and entered the judgment room. He also stayed there a long time and did not return.

When the door opened for the third time, the invitation to enter was extended to the man in the next chair. "Would Michael Wilcox, the father of Megan Wilcox, please come forward and render an account of his stewardship?"

The invitations were extended in sequence, relative to each of my children. As I watched, the father of Benjamin Wilcox, then of Cade Wilcox, and finally of McKay Wilcox entered the judgment room.

I received the distinct impression in this pondering that if I could answer well for my efforts in those first six chairs and the seventh, which was Michael Wilcox, the son of Norma Wilcox, I could feel confident and calm about appearing before my Father in Heaven some time in the future when the accounting was real. It was a profoundly instructive moment for me on the importance of my relationship and efforts with each of my children separately.

## GIVING MUSCLE TO PARENT WORDS

As we examine Alma's words to Helaman, we are immediately introduced to what we might call "parent words," just as we saw testimony words used earlier. Alma tells Helaman, "I would that ye should do" (Alma 36:2). As mothers and fathers we often use words like *would* or *want* or *should*. "I *want* you to pick up your toys," or "You *should* clean your room." These types of sentences are everyday occurrences.

Later, we see Alma using another common parental expression:

"Ye . . . ought to retain in remembrance. . . . Ye ought to know" (Alma 36:29–30). *Ought* and *remember* are used as frequently as *would* and *should*. Perhaps the strongest parent word Alma employs is "I *command* you" (Alma 37:1; emphasis added). Similar words are used with Shiblon in Alma 38 and Corianton in Alma 39.

What gives muscle or validity to such words? Notice that almost every time Alma uses these types of expressions he follows them up with, "as I have done," or another phrase suitable to the situation. Even when he commands his son Corianton to return and "acknowledge your faults and that wrong which ye have done" to the Zoramites (Alma 39:13), we know from Alma's earlier life that he and the repentant sons of Mosiah also "traveled throughout all the land . . . zealously striving to repair all the injuries which they had done to the church" (Mosiah 27:35).

Parental example is such an obvious necessity that it hardly needs elaboration. When we say "you should" or "we would" or "you ought" or "I command," our children need to know that we can follow up those words with "as I have." That does not mean we actually say the words every time, as that would prove rather annoying for a child and could be alienating, but our sons and daughters need to realize that the words can be said because the actions of the parent in his own life match his wishes for the child.

I believe that is what the Prophet Joseph Smith meant when he spoke of the qualities of priesthood leadership in Doctrine and Covenants 121. There he says that influence can be maintained only "without hypocrisy, and without guile" (v. 42). This same idea is implied in Enos's evaluation of his father when he wrote: "I, Enos, knowing my father that he was a just man" (Enos 1:1). Justice, as a parental trait, does not expect of the child that which the mother or father is not also living. We may equally suppose that this thought is contained in Nephi's initial words that he had "been born of goodly parents" (1 Nephi 1:1).

## GREAT THINGS REQUIRED OF THEIR FATHERS

I recall one afternoon, while preparing a lesson for an institute class, I took a few moments from my studies to watch my youngest son playing with his trucks. He saw me sitting with my scriptures open and a red pencil in my hand. He dropped his trucks, ran to his bedroom, where he retrieved his own paperback copy of the Book of Mormon and a pencil, and returned. He sat next to me, opened his Book of Mormon, and began to underline. As I watched this, the Lord taught me a sobering lesson. "Do you understand how great your influence is at this most crucial time in your son's eternal journey?"

I was so grateful that it was my scripture study my son was emulating at that moment. There are other things in my life that I would not have been as happy to see repeated in my child. Now, I realize that the Lord could intervene with his own influence, but he rarely intrudes on the agency he has bestowed upon us. Early in the Restoration the Lord spoke of this when he indicated the innocence of little children: "For it is given unto them even as I will, according to mine own pleasure, that great things may be required at the hand of their fathers" (D&C 29:48).

When my first child was born, I was extremely nervous about being a good father. The natural apprehension we all feel as our children come was augmented in my situation by the fact that I had not been raised by a father myself, so I had no example to follow. I had a wonderful mother, but I had never seen, in an intimate manner, how a father acted in a family. I petitioned the Lord to show me the way, for I was deeply fearful that I would do everything wrong and bring tragedy and sorrow upon my children.

It was with these feelings that I sat in sacrament meeting one Sunday in the Southern California chapel where I had attended church while growing up. My daughter was about six months old, and I was wrestling with her as the deacons began to pass the sacrament. Someone had suggested to me that a good way to think about the Savior while struggling with a wiggling child was to imagine Jesus with the children.

One of my favorite chapters in the scriptures is 3 Nephi 17. Here the Savior asks the Nephite parents to bring their little children to him. I began to reflect on that scene. In my mind I was there in Bountiful with the other parents. I was holding my infant daughter as the Savior asked for the little children to be brought to him. Everyone cleared a path as the parents took the children to Jesus. The scriptures tell us that "he took their little children, one by one, and blessed them, and prayed unto the Father for them" (3 Nephi 17:21).

I listened to the blessings and prayers. They contained all that I could ever hope for in the life of my own daughter. Wonderful promises were given relating to their future lives of righteousness, fulfillment, and joy. I thought as I listened, "If I can just place my daughter in the arms of the Savior, he will grant her a similar blessing and prayer, which will carry her through life. It won't matter how good a father I am. His prayerful blessing of her will compensate for all my mistakes and weaknesses."

I awaited an opportunity, and soon he looked in my direction. He read my thoughts and knew what I wanted. With a gentle gesture he held out his hands to take my daughter into his arms. I crossed the few steps between us and with deep gratitude and immense relief placed her in his hands. All would now be well. He embraced her for a few moments of private contemplation, then, holding her up in his two hands and looking directly into my face, with his eyes open, he blessed my daughter. These were his words: "I bless you, Kirsten, that you will walk in the footsteps of your father, and become as he is." Then he smiled and returned my daughter to me. I took her and walked away much sobered.

I knew what the message was. It was as if he said, "Don't pass on to me your responsibility to this child, young father. If you wish her to be faithful, you be faithful. If you wish her to live the gospel, you live the gospel. If you desire her to pray, to love the scriptures and the temple, you do the same. She will follow you. You will set the pace. You will establish the direction."

I left sacrament meeting that morning humbled but empowered.

## CHAPTER SEVEN

But continue thou in the things which thou hast learned
and hast been assured of, knowing of whom thou hast
learned them; and that from a child thou hast known the
holy scriptures, which are able to make thee wise unto
salvation through faith which is in Christ Jesus.
*2 Timothy 3:14–15*

# Enlarging the Memory

## THE ROD, THE SWORD, THE COMPASS

When Lehi related his dream of the tree of life to his family he spoke of the significant role the iron rod played in getting people to the tree. When Nephi later explained that the iron rod represented the word of God and testified of its importance to his brothers, he said, "Whoso . . . would hold fast unto it, they would never perish; neither could the temptations and the fiery darts of the adversary overpower them unto blindness, to lead them away" (1 Nephi 15:24).

What a marvelous promise relative to the power of the scriptures.

Mormon later gave a similar assurance, saying, "Whosoever will may lay hold upon the word of God, which is quick and powerful, which shall divide asunder all the cunning and the snares and the wiles of the devil, and lead the man of Christ in a strait and narrow course . . . and land their souls, yea, their immortal souls, at the right hand of God in the kingdom of heaven, to sit down with

Abraham, and Isaac, and with Jacob, and with all our holy fathers, to go no more out" (Helaman 3:29-30).

Is this not what we all want for our children? The scriptures are an iron rod running along the bank of a dangerous, threatening river. "Don't send your children along the riverbank of life without a good grip on the iron rod," the Lord teaches us. "They will fall in and drown." The scriptures are a sword "quick and powerful," and life is a battle. "Don't send your children into the battles of life without placing the sword in their hands—they will be defeated," the Lord cautions.

We can examine other metaphorical portraits of the scriptures, and they all give the same message. In the Old Testament the scriptures are "a lamp unto my feet, and a light unto my path" (Psalm 119:105). "Don't send your children into a world of darkness without giving them a lamp to light their way," our Father in Heaven urges. "They will stumble and lose their way." The scriptures are manna, the bread from heaven God has given to nourish us through life (see Deuteronomy 8:3). "Don't send your children across the desert of mortality without teaching them to harvest the manna each day—they will starve."

In the direction Alma the Younger gave his son Helaman, he stressed the importance of the scriptures, using the Liahona as a metaphor. "It was prepared to show unto our fathers the course which they should travel in the wilderness. And it did work for them according to their faith in God; therefore, if they had faith to believe that God could cause that those spindles should point the way they should go, behold, it was done." When they became "slothful" or "forgot to exercise their faith . . . they did not progress in their journey" (Alma 37:39-41).

Life is a wilderness and the scriptures are our compass. "Don't send your children into the wilderness without giving them a compass—they will get lost," the Lord says. If we have faith that the stories, examples, speeches, parables, and doctrines of the scriptures can point our way in life it will be done. As Alma taught this to Helaman, he specifically pointed out the things the scriptures will do for those who search them. "They have enlarged the memory of this people," he maintained (Alma 37:8).

An enlarged memory is just the thing to give our sons and daughters. In truth, the scriptures' first title suggested this very idea. If we turn to the Pearl of Great Price we learn that "a book of remembrance was kept, . . . for it was given unto as many as called upon God to write by the spirit of inspiration; and by them their children were taught to read and write, having a language which was pure and undefiled" (Moses 6:5-6). The scriptures were called a "book of remembrance" in the earliest ages of the world. The very name implies that the Lord wishes us to remember the things contained therein. They are worthy of remembering!

Later, Enoch spoke of the importance of this book of remembrance: "And death hath come upon our fathers; nevertheless *we know them*, and cannot deny, and even the first of all we know, even Adam. For a book of remembrance we have written among us, according to the pattern given by the finger of God; and it is given in our own language" (Moses 6:45-46; emphasis added).

Notice that the wording of the verse is not that we can know *about* the great men and women of the scriptures, but we can *know* them. There is a force associated with the Lord's book of remembrance, an energy which enables us to enter into the minds, hearts, and lives of some of the noblest souls who have lived, to make them our friends. There are so few heroes in the world today to which we can direct our children's attention. The scriptures provide them.

## MAKING FRIENDS IN HISTORY

When I was in junior high school and high school, my friends were essential to me. I have sometimes referred to this time of life as the "friend worship" stage of existence. We usually try to imitate the things or people we worship. It can be a dangerous time for children, especially when friends exert unwanted influence. Improper behavior may be imitated. In college I also associated with some very close friends. After high school I rarely saw any of my old friends. We went to college, to work, to the rest of our lives, and lost track of each other. The same thing happened in college. With very few exceptions, I do not continue to see or associate with my old friends. How tragic it would have been had I done something regrettable because of the peer pressure of friends I would not see again after a very short time.

During those formative years, however, my mother introduced me to another set of friends, those in the scriptures, those whom the Lord wishes us all to remember. Here Nephi, Moses, Peter, Esther, Rebekah, Abraham, and, above all, Jesus become our companions. We meet very few people in life as remarkable, as intelligent, as righteous, and as wonderfully human as those we find in the standard works. Over the years, these friends in the scriptures will go with us. We can become more and more deeply acquainted with them. They will open their hearts and minds to us. As Moses 6 promises, we can "know them" (Moses 6:45). Our children will make friends in school and church without needing much help from us. As parents we may have little power in determining those friends. Let us make sure, however, that they are introduced to the best friends they can have—eternal friends they will one day meet in person, as Mormon promised when he said the scriptures would "land their souls . . . at the right hand of God," to sit down with "all our holy fathers" (Helaman 3:30).

My love for these friends was instilled in my soul by my

mother's voice. Even when I was small she read the scriptural stories to me. She chose her stories by adapting them to the age and
maturity of my sisters and me. I remember her telling the accounts
of Samson, the boy Samuel hearing the voice of God, David and
Goliath, Daniel and the lions, the parables of Jesus, and Nephi
building the ship. Even a tiny child can understand these stories.

Because they were first introduced to me by my mother, whom
I trusted and loved, they became a deep part of me. Their truths will
always be mingled with the affection I had and have for my mother.
We must read to our children, everything from children's literature
(which tends to remain very moral in character) to the standard
works, but especially the standard works.

Arthur Henry King, perhaps the finest teacher I ever had, wrote
a poem about living a vicarious life with seers, prophets, and the
Savior. "This man loved reading," he wrote, "his neighbors were all
ghosts, and he spent his life seeing them."[1]

There is a wonderful statement made by a Chinese philosopher
named Mencius about this type of friendship. He spoke of the most
virtuous men in a village seeking the friendship of other virtuous
men in the village. Not content, they then proceeded to make
friends with the most virtuous individuals in the province and then
continued on to make friends with the most virtuous people in the
whole kingdom. At that point they "proceed[ed] to ascend to consider the men of antiquity." They studied their words, their lives,
and the times in which they lived. "This is to ascend and make
friends of the men of antiquity."[2] Another translation from the
Chinese states it simply: "This is to make friends in history."

I love the idea inherent in Mencius's term that we "ascend"
when we turn to the past to find friends. This is, without question,

true of scriptural heroes. How vitally important to help our children ascend and make friends in history.

## FATHER BENJAMIN BEFORE KING BENJAMIN

The life of Alma the Younger concludes with our view of him as a father, and our introduction to King Benjamin allows us to see him as a father before he climbs his famous tower to give that soul-shaking address. As a father, like Alma, Benjamin stressed the importance of the scriptures to his three sons. "And he caused that they should be taught in all the language of his fathers," in order to read the scriptural accounts. He then taught what we can anticipate the scriptures will do for our children. Among other things they will enable them to "become men [and women] of understanding." They will prevent them from "suffer[ing] in ignorance . . . not knowing the mysteries of God." They enable us to "have his commandments always before our eyes." They will prevent them from dwindling in unbelief. Benjamin then testified to their truth, saying, "These sayings are true. . . . and we can know of their surety." He concluded with these words: "And now, my sons, I would that ye should remember to search them diligently, that ye may profit thereby" (Mosiah 1:2–3, 5–7).

Each of Benjamin's purposes could be discussed, but let me illustrate the power of just one of Benjamin's reasons. Years ago, my wife's aunt was sitting in a bus station when another woman sat down near her and began to weep. Because my wife's aunt is a compassionate woman, she slid next to the weeping woman and asked her if she could do anything for her.

The woman replied, "My baby is dead!" This engendered a long conversation in which my wife's aunt tried to console her new friend, but nothing she said had any effect. Over and over again she heard the same words, "My baby is dead!"

Finally she asked her when her child had died and received the answer that it had been ten years previous. "Why do you still grieve so deeply and with such absence of hope?" she asked.

"Because I did not baptize my daughter before she died," the woman replied. "I knew I needed to do it, but I delayed, and now my priest has told me my baby can't go to heaven. It is entirely my fault."

There was no question this woman was suffering. The loss of a child is a dear thing to endure, but her suffering was intensified by ignorance. She was suffering in ignorance because she did not know the mysteries of God. Within a few minutes she could be shown scriptures in both the Book of Mormon and the Doctrine and Covenants that would heal that suffering.

This is only one example. We could call upon many more. The deeper our understanding of the Lord's book of remembrance, the less likely we are to suffer in ignorance. Life will be difficult enough for our sons and daughters without the added sorrow of suffering that need never be endured.

## ARM THEM FOR A LIFETIME

The importance of an enlarged memory was forcefully demonstrated to me when my daughter went to Russia to teach English. The Soviet Union had just fallen; e-mail and telephone communication with her would be very difficult. She was barely out of high school, but my wife and I felt this would be a wonderful opportunity for her. The Church was not yet established there. While in Russia, she was invited to listen to a professor of great scholarship. As he talked in an informal setting with my daughter and some of her friends, he challenged their faith. He was very persuasive, and his arguments were difficult for such young and untrained minds to combat.

My daughter grew more and more uncomfortable and yet was

unable to resist the logic of what he was saying. "I kept thinking," she told me later, "that what he was saying sounded so familiar. I couldn't place it, but my mind was racing to find out why I thought I had heard all this before. Suddenly it came; he was teaching the same things Korihor taught in Alma. I almost jumped up and pointed at him, saying, 'Korihor, I know you! You're Korihor!' After that I felt fine and no longer feared what he was saying. He was not new to me. I knew his type from the scriptures."

To instill a confidence and love for the scriptures in a child is to arm that child for a lifetime. It is to surround him or her with great men and women, and it is a law of life that we tend to become like those with whom we choose to keep company. If we teach a child to read—a talent all will agree is vital and necessary—without teaching what is worth reading, we have done the child no favor. We may actually do harm, for there is much written in society that is damaging and soul-shaking to read. Let our children have a standard to guide them. The enlarging of their memory gives them access to six thousand years of courage, wisdom, compassion, and faith—God's standard.

C. S. Lewis stated: "A man who has lived in many places is not likely to be deceived by the local errors of his native village: the scholar has lived in many times and is therefore in some degree immune from the great cataract of nonsense that pours from the press and the microphone of his own age."[3] As Alma explained to Helaman, the scriptures have "convinced many of the error of their ways." They are also good at revealing "incorrect tradition[s]" (Alma 37:8, 9). Of all the things a parent could put into the hands or mind of a child, an ability to wield the sword of the word, or follow the directions of that compass, or grasp tightly to the iron rod, is indispensable.

⌒

## CHAPTER EIGHT

*My beloved son, Moroni, . . . I am mindful of you always*
*in my prayers, continually praying unto God the Father*
*in the name of his Holy Child, Jesus, that he, through his*
*infinite goodness and grace, will keep you through the*
*endurance of faith on his name to the end.*
*Moroni 8:2–3*

# Praise and Validation

## "I HAVE HAD GREAT JOY IN THEE"

As a father, Jacob experienced both the highs and the lows of a parent. He had the joy, despair, and then joy again in his son Joseph. Jacob had twelve sons, who became the main branches of the tree we call the house of Israel, yet their behavior as described in Genesis is not particularly exemplary. At the end of his long life he gave each a patriarchal blessing. These blessings are very brief, and though we may not have Jacob's complete words, I have learned from them, particularly Reuben's blessing.

Reuben, you will remember, defiled Bilhah, Jacob's wife, at the death of Rachel. There are different reasons discussed for this strange act of Reuben, but whatever the reason, he lost blessings because of it. Yet, in Jacob's last words, he still found reason to praise his eldest son. "Reuben, thou art my firstborn, my might, and the beginning of my strength, the excellency of dignity, and the excellency of power" (Genesis 49:3). The blessing continues by referencing his past decision, but there is no question that Jacob's first words show his love and recognition of his son's strengths. Children need to be praised, even though, as in this case, there can be much to criticize.

If we search Alma's words to his second son, Shiblon, we find this parental quality displayed with much affection. "My son, I trust that *I shall have great joy in you,* because of your steadiness and your faithfulness unto God." Perhaps at this point Alma paused, looked at his son, and decided to change the tense of his praise from future to past. It is a slight change, but I think it is very revealing. "I say unto you, my son, that *I have had great joy in thee already,* because of thy faithfulness and thy diligence, and thy patience" (Alma 38:2, 3; emphasis added). Alma continues by referring to these qualities as they were displayed among the Zoramites. In other words, the praise was not only generous but specific.

We often tell our children how good they are. It seems this praise is more effective when directed to particular identifiable accomplishments, character traits, or abilities. We can learn from Alma's words to Shiblon to tell our children not only that we love them, which is often done, but also how much joy they give us. Alma directed his praise to the happiness his son's character and growth had given him. And he expressed his assurance that it would continue into the future. I can remember many times when my mother praised me, and she told me she loved me every day, yet the one time that means the most to me and lives deepest in my memory is when she simply said, "I can't tell you how happy I am when I think that you are my son." Perhaps "I love you" and "I'm proud of you" are used so often that the expression of joy in a child, because it is different and seldom said, at least in my experience, resonates to a different chord.

In the middle of a letter sent to Moroni from his father, Mormon, and preserved by Moroni, we read of a simple yet endearing moment of praise. "Behold, my son, I cannot recommend them [his people, the Nephites] unto God lest he should smite me. But behold, my son, I recommend thee unto God, and I trust in Christ that thou wilt be saved" (Moroni 9:21–22). These were difficult times for father and son, but there is no question as we read the letters treasured by Moroni that there was an abiding bond woven between them. Much of its strength came from the calm assurance Moroni received that he was pleasing to his father.

## "THIS IS MY BELOVED SON"

In truth, do we not see this quality beautifully portrayed by our Father in Heaven each time he speaks of his Son? To those gathered among the ruins of Bountiful, the Father introduced his Son with "Behold my Beloved Son, in whom I am well pleased, in whom I have glorified my name" (3 Nephi 11:7). On the Mount of Transfiguration, Peter, James, and John heard the voice of the Father praising his Son: "This is my beloved Son, in whom I am well pleased" (Matthew 17:5). Speaking of this moment years later, Peter remembered, "He received from God the Father honour and glory" (2 Peter 1:17). We hear these same words uttered by the Father at the Savior's baptism (see Matthew 3:17). To the kneeling Joseph Smith in the Sacred Grove, the Father again spoke of his joy and pleasure in his Son. "This is My Beloved Son. Hear Him!" (JS–H 1:17). Nephi testified that he "heard a voice from the Father, saying: Yea, the words of my Beloved are true and faithful" (2 Nephi 31:15).

Part of the wonder of God's practice of praising was taught by

Jesus in a very simple phrase. He knew his Father's ways and encouraged us all when he said, "Whosoever shall give to drink unto one of these little ones a cup of cold water only in the name of a disciple, verily I say unto you, he shall in no wise lose his reward" (Matthew 10:42). We worship a Father who notices even the tiniest of kindnesses. There is no simpler act of service that can be done than giving a child a drink of water, yet even this is noted by the Father and rewarded. In our own relationships, it is well when we notice the small kindnesses of our children and then praise and reward those tiny acts. In this manner we may find an infinite number of opportunities to praise a child.

## VALIDATING GOODNESS

Commending a child may also contain a validation of the child's goodness, decisions, or acts. Alma mentions some of the persecutions Shiblon suffered while teaching the Zoramites, praising his patience in enduring them. Then he adds the following validation: "Thou didst bear all these things with patience because the Lord was with thee; *and now thou knowest that the Lord did deliver thee*" (Alma 38:4; emphasis added). Validation confirms to a child the truth of experiences shared or learned. Children often do not know the full significance of certain events or moments in their lives. This gives the parent the opportunity to endorse the tutorial nature of various occurrences in their lives and offer support if needed.

I recall such a moment in my son's life. We had gone to the temple so he could participate for the first time in being baptized for the dead in behalf of his ancestors. During the confirmations he had a truly remarkable experience with those ancestors. When the session was over he asked if he could talk with me. We sat in a corner by ourselves, and he shared his first major encounter with spiritual truth. Then, in a tone of twelve-year-old hesitant humility, he asked if I thought it was from his Father in Heaven. I knew even as he was sharing it that the Holy Spirit had granted my son a beautiful testimony about the relevancy of temple work, the thinness of the veil, and the love and gratitude that flows when the hearts of the fathers and children turn toward each other.

Yet he, at age twelve, did not understand the significance of what had happened nor the gift that had been bestowed. He needed validation, and what wonderful moments we shared as I was able to assure him that his experience was indeed from God. Similar substantiation often needs to be given to support children when they make important decisions or when they wrestle with right and wrong. Remember, we are here to learn how to differentiate between the two.

We see a great example of validation in Joseph Smith's history recorded in the Pearl of Great Price and in the biography written about him by his mother, Lucy Mack Smith. The morning after Joseph had his three consecutive conversations with Moroni, he was working in the field when his father noticed he was exhausted. He was sent home but fainted while attempting to climb a fence. When he revived, Moroni was again at his side. "The first thing he said was, 'Why did you not tell your father that which I commanded you to tell him?' Joseph replied, 'I was afraid my father would not believe me.' The angel rejoined, 'He will believe every word you say to him.'"[1]

In Joseph's version of this same event, we read: "He . . . commanded me to go to my father and tell him of the vision and commandments which I had received. I obeyed; I returned to my father in the field, and rehearsed the whole matter to him. He replied to me that it was of God, and told me to go and do as commanded by the messenger" (JS–H 1:49–50).

The visitations of the previous night were important enough for Joseph to tell his father about that Moroni instructed him by way of a commandment, not a suggestion. And Moroni anticipated it would be done immediately—the first thing the next morning. We might ponder why this was so important. Joseph would receive critical support from his family throughout his life, and in the field that morning he received important validation of his visions as expressed in his father's belief and exhortation to do as he was commanded. It must have been comforting indeed for the young Joseph Smith to hear his father tell him that all he had experienced "was of God." With this assurance sounding in his heart, Joseph went to the Hill Cumorah.

~

## CHAPTER NINE

And all thy children shall be taught of the Lord;
and great shall be the peace of thy children.
*Isaiah 54:13*

# Nurture and Admonition

## THE CRITICAL BALANCE

Generally we think of the book of Enos in the context of prayer, but if we look a little more closely we will see some amazing truths relative to influencing a child positively. Enos begins by praising his father as he reflects on Jacob's actions toward him. "I, Enos, knowing my father that he was a just man—for he taught me in his language, and also in the nurture and admonition of the Lord—and blessed be the name of my God for it" (Enos 1:1).

There are a number of key words we could examine here that give a parent insight, such as *just* and *taught*, but let us focus on *nurture* and *admonition*. A remarkable and critical balance is depicted in these two words that is necessary if we are to achieve the results we desire with our children. Sometimes I ask my classes at the University of Utah Institute of Religion to give me all the words and phrases they can think of when I say the word *nurture*. They come up with *care, cherish, love, support, look out for, foster, protect, compassion.* I then ask them which parent, mother or father, in their own experience is most closely associated with the idea of nurture. Almost without exception, they answer, "Mother." It is interesting that all the words associated in our minds with the concept of nurturing are positive, warm, and welcoming. We all desire to be nurtured. Praising a child is a form of nurturing that fosters growth.

I then do the same thing with the word *admonition.* Once again I ask my students to give me all the words that come to mind when they think of receiving admonition. The words they recite are *encourage, discipline, warn, exhort, caution, reprove, reprimand,* and *teach.* Which parent most often comes to mind when we think of the need for admonition? Almost without deviation, they answer, "Father."

Now, fathers can nurture and mothers admonish, but there seems to be a balance in the normal structures of the nuclear family between nurture and admonition, provided by the differing qualities men and women bring to a marriage. I was raised by a single mother, so she had to do both the nurturing and the admonishing. Many other families likewise do not fit the traditional mode. What is important to realize is the need for both nurture and admonition in the raising of a child. Enos received both in his upbringing and was duly grateful.

What may be the result if a child receives only nurturing without the counterbalance of admonition? They may become manipulative, spoiled, self-centered, and unprepared for the world, for the world is not often a nurturing place. What may be the result if a child receives an overload of admonition without the softer stimulus of nurture? We may find them insecure, timid, unsure of themselves, or rebellious, taciturn, contrary.

The apostle Paul gave the same counsel in two of his epistles, centering his counsel on the actions of fathers and a tendency they may have to over-admonish. To the Ephesians he wrote: "Fathers, provoke not your children to wrath: but bring them up in the nurture and admonition of the Lord" (Ephesians 6:4). In his epistle to the Colossians he pointed out another response of a child to a hand too heavy in admonition: "Fathers, provoke not your children to anger, lest they become discouraged" (Colossians 3:21).

We desire neither wrath nor discouragement in our sons and daughters. Nurture provides the balance.

Another factor seems to fit nicely in the scale of nurture and admonition. Experience shows us that nurture tends to lend itself to the more immediate needs of a child. It deals mostly with the present. In saying this I do not mean it is not crucial for the future development of a child but rather that it responds in the here and now. Admonition usually has a future perspective inherent in it. Admonition faces coming events and seeks to prepare the child, either by initiating a change or offering counsel or warning. In my own family life, I frequently find my wife, in her nurturing role, concerned about solving a problem, soothing a child, or attending to a worry that needs attention right away. I often find my own thoughts directed to the future consequences of responding to a child or helping him or her face a challenge. A small, everyday example may help to illustrate. If one of my children forgets his lunch, my wife will be the first to say, "I'd better run it right down to the school for him." My response is more likely to be, "Missing a lunch won't kill him, and tomorrow he won't forget it."

We must also recognize that each child is unique. That uniqueness demands that the balance between nurture and admonition be adjusted accordingly. Some children need more nurture because their personality demands it. Some children may need a little more admonition, depending on their character. Sometimes the differences our children notice in how we respond to them in comparison to our responses to their siblings are because of this balance. They may perceive they are getting more than their share of admonition while a sister or brother is receiving primarily nurture. The important thing is that they know, as Enos did, that their parents are just, or trying their best to be so. It is also essential that each child receive both the needed nurture and proper admonition, even though these may be administered in varying degrees.

President Brigham Young applied the nurture/admonition principle to us all when he said, "You may, figuratively speaking, pound one Elder over the head with a club, and he does not know but what you have handed him a straw dipped in molasses to suck. There are others, if you speak a word to them, or take a straw and chasten them, whose hearts are broken; they are as tender in their feelings as an infant, and will melt like wax before the flame. You must not chasten them severely; you must chasten according to the spirit that is in the person. . . . There is a great variety. Treat people as they are."[1]

## "THE JOY OF THE SAINTS"

Jacob's role as a parent gives us further food for thought. Enos indicated that while he was hunting beasts in the forest, "the words which I had *often* heard my father speak concerning eternal life, and *the joy of the saints,* sunk deep into my heart. And my soul hungered" (Enos 1:3–4; emphasis added).

I am impressed that it was "the joy of the saints" that struck Enos. It was the positive, happy truths of the gospel for which he sought. This is one of the best ways to nurture a child. Depending upon how it is presented, the gospel may be perceived either as a barbed wire fence keeping us away from all the good green grass on the other side or as the loving arms of a Father in Heaven anxious for his children's welfare.

Children must see the "glad tidings," the cheer-inspiring, soul-rejoicing qualities the Lord has provided for their lives. It was the optimistic, affirmative, encouraging forces of the Lord's plan of happiness Enos wanted, for these were the things his father "often" spoke about.

We most frequently call the Lord's plan the plan of salvation. This is appropriate and good, but in the Book of Mormon it has other, equally compelling names. In Alma 42, Alma the Younger identifies it as "the great plan of salvation" (v. 5), "the great plan of happiness" (v. 8), "the plan of redemption" (vv. 11, 13), and "the plan of mercy" (v. 15). I personally prefer "the great plan of happiness" or "plan of mercy," but we seldom call it by these names, preferring "salvation" instead. "Plan of salvation" always directs my thoughts to diagrams on the blackboard complete with circles and lines. I think in linear terms stretching back into the past and forward into the future, a progression, but not an emotional state. "Plan of happiness" suggests a manner of living, an affirmation of the present which draws from the past and projects optimistically into the future.

Regardless of what we call it, may we present its commandments, counsels, ordinances, doctrines, and principles in the joy they profess to create. Remember that the fruit of the tree of life in Lehi's dream was "desirable" specifically because it made "one happy" (1 Nephi 8:10). King Benjamin encouraged his people by inviting them to "consider on the blessed and happy state of those that keep the commandments of God. . . . If they hold out faithful to the end they are received into heaven, that thereby they may dwell with God in a state of never-ending happiness" (Mosiah 2:41). Abraham discovered there was "greater happiness" and "sought" the blessings that would bring it (Abraham 1:2). Even a cursory examination of the Doctrine and Covenants reveals that in at least a third of its sections we are told to rejoice, be glad, be cheerful, and experience joy and happiness. The scriptural assurances of this are almost endless.

## "A TIME TO LAUGH"

At various times throughout religious history, there has seemed to be a resistance to cheerful joy, almost as if there were a distrust of human pleasure. "Can it be righteous and acceptable to God if it is enjoyable?" was the frequent question. I have never understood this distrust and, sometimes, outright hostility. Even in Ecclesiastes we are told there is "a time to laugh . . . and a time to dance" (Ecclesiastes 3:4). Laughter and play are part of the gospel. The happiness and joy we have spoken of need not always be cosmic and eternal in scope; it can be quite ordinary. "A merry heart maketh a cheerful countenance," wrote Solomon, and he added, "A merry heart doeth good like a medicine" (Proverbs 15:13; 17:22). We have relegated "merry" to Christmas. The word suggests a celebratory joy, but a merry, holiday hope-filled heart is a year-long necessity. We are created in the image of God, certainly physically, but also our personalities and character. God is merciful; therefore, mercy is part of the human soul. Whatever we find positive in ourselves must have its origin in God. He must have an open and delightful sense of humor, for we appreciate and love this quality in others. The ability to laugh lightheartedly with our children is part of the joy of the gospel they need to feel.

I recall a conversation I had once with the wife of one of my cousins. I was playing a game of kick-the-can with her children and my own. "Your mother taught you to play and laugh," she commented. "My husband didn't learn that in his childhood. It was all chores and work. I should very much like to see him playing games with our children."

That caused me to think. My wife and I decided we wanted to

share laughter and fun with our children in a gospel setting. For instance, we wanted our children to "call the sabbath a delight," as Isaiah said (Isaiah 58:13), and not see it as overly restrictive. We used the television as an ally, not an enemy. Movies could be watched as long as we watched together and the movie was edifying. Sunday movies were special ones. We went through all the musicals, and such classics as *Ben Hur* and *The Ten Commandments*. To this day some of our children's favorite movies are "the Sunday movies."

Home evenings always included a game of some sort which we invented. We had to be creative over the years, and not everything worked smoothly, but such activities as Pumpkin Bowling at Halloween became traditional, as did Lehi Legos (Book of Mormon stories acted out on a Lego stage with Lego people), and Scriptural Treasure Hunts. It is so gratifying to hear our children, who are now adults, laughing and reminiscing around the kitchen table when we gather for holidays or special events. Laughter is part of the gospel! It is part of eternity!

## "OFTEN"

Jacob "often" spoke of "the joy of the saints" (Enos 1:3). Testimony or faith needs to be given weight so it may sink deep into the soul of a child and create the hunger Enos speaks about. I picture the soul of a child as the smooth surface of a deep lake. As parents, we want the truths and teachings of eternity to sink deep within that lake. Mothers and fathers float truths out onto the surface with the hope they will sink into the heart of the child. By floating them out "often," we give weight to those teachings. As they pile up on each other, weight is created, until by force of their frequency they sink into the child's heart. Weight can be given to faith in a number of ways. Sacrifice, for instance, creates that necessary weight; speaking "often" of important truths is equally effective in forming the needed emphasis. That is I how I perceive it.

A caution may be in order here. We need to be careful of overemphasis that becomes mere redundancy, but Jacob's emphasis obviously had the desired effect. In response, Enos hungered, crying out for the satisfaction of that hunger, and the Lord took over from there. Will he not also do that for our children if we float truths out onto the surface often enough?

## OF EVERY TREE THOU MAYEST FREELY EAT

One of the earliest lessons we learn in the scriptures occurs in the Garden of Eden in the first counsels given to Adam and Eve. It is a marvelous lesson from our Eternal Father in Heaven about life and how to present it to our children. Notice how positive he was when he spoke to Adam: "Of every tree of the garden thou mayest freely eat, but of the tree of the knowledge of good and evil, thou shalt not eat of it" (Moses 3:16–17).

I used to picture the first great choice given to man as being between two trees—the tree of life and the tree of the knowledge of good and evil. But if we read carefully, we immediately see that the choice was between the many trees of the garden they could "freely" partake of and a single tree that was off-limits. In light of all the things they could do and could partake of, one restriction would not seem too prohibitive. We are being taught a proper approach to life at the very beginning of man's participation in it. If we spend our lives focused on all the things we do have and can do, we will live happy, contented, productive, and grateful lives. God would have us live in this manner, for there are many decent, wholesome, edifying things available even in our ofttimes decadent, decaying world.

Here is a wondrous approach for a father or mother. Let us help our children focus on all they can do and all they have, and let us point them out as well as provide these things for them. I wish I had learned this earlier. It would have helped me in even the most casual demands of parenting. Too often I found myself saying, "Don't touch Daddy's stereo," rather than, "You can play with anything else in the house you like, but please don't touch Daddy's stereo."

Lucifer then enters the garden. Notice his approach. "Yea, hath God said—Ye shall not eat of every tree of the garden?" (Moses 4:7). The adversary wished them to focus on the one tree of which they could not freely partake. So it is in life. He still wishes us to center our attention on those things we do not have and cannot partake of. If we live our lives in this manner we will be discontented, feverish, unsatisfied, ungrateful, and rebellious.

It may be a temptation for parents as they raise their families to focus too much on the "forbidden things" rather than on the things we can "freely" partake of. Centering our attention on the positive helps create a joy in life in general as well as a joy in the gospel. If one movie is not up to our standards, can we not point out ten that are? If one fashion is questionable, are there not five that would be acceptable?

Part of the secret of life is being able ourselves to perceive the world in this manner and help our children to perceive it in a similar fashion. This also necessitates our own awareness of the many trees available. As Article of Faith 13 specifies, we must "seek after" things that are "virtuous, lovely, or of good report or praiseworthy." Then we invite our sons and daughters to "freely" partake of them. Lehi had to first taste the fruit of the tree of life and know that it was sweet and "desirable above all other fruit" before he "beckoned" to his family to "come unto me, and partake of the fruit" (1 Nephi 8:12–15). That is a parent's job. That is a parent's opportunity.

⌒

## CHAPTER TEN

*That they may prepare the minds of their children
to hear the word at the time of his coming.*
*Alma 39:16*

# Creating an Environment

## "UPON THE POSTS OF THY HOUSE"

One of the most sobering moments as a parent came to me the day my oldest daughter first went to kindergarten. It was really an unremarkable incident, but it shook me to the core. The morning was exciting as she put on new school clothes and proudly carried her book bag to school. I thought nothing of this new adventure in her life until she came home that night and related to me something she had learned that day. I do not remember what it was she told me. It was not something wrong or anything that caused me concern, but it was something neither I nor her mother had taught her. I realized with a certain shock that my daughter would increasingly come under the influence of people and events I could neither control nor safeguard her against.

It was a sobering moment. What would happen when she was taught something wrong or challenging to her faith or to the moral standard we were creating in our home? I determined then that as much as I could I would make sure she received all the goodness her mother and I could give her in the hope it would fortify her for those things over which we had no control. The environment we did have some command of would be positive.

In Moses' epic final address to his people, he counseled parents to teach their children to love the Lord with all their heart, soul, and might and to serve him. The great truths he had brought down from Sinai would be the foundation stones upon which their children's lives should be built. "And thou shalt teach them diligently unto thy children," he told them, "and shalt talk of them when thou sittest in thine house, and when thou walkest by the way, and when thou liest down, and when thou risest up. And thou shalt bind them for a sign upon thine hand, and they shall be as frontlets between thine eyes. And thou shalt write them upon the posts of thy house, and on thy gates" (Deuteronomy 6:7-9).

This counsel is repeated in Deuteronomy 11:18-20, highlighting its importance. Not only was Moses emphasizing the need of frequency of teaching, as we have already discussed, but it seems as if he was telling his people to be deeply aware of the environment surrounding their children. They were going into a Canaanite world where many influences would tear at the continuity of God's teachings. It was a hostile moral atmosphere and needed to be offset by the active creation of an opposite setting, one conducive to growth towards righteousness. A barrier between that Canaanite world and their children was necessary, and the parents were to fashion it. Goodness and truth and beauty were to be the topic of discussion. They would be constantly before the eyes of the family and on the posts of their homes, surrounding them, cushioning them, inviting them to a higher standard. In the home they had power. This was their domain, one resistant to the invasions of godlessness. Here was an environment they could command without the distracting influence of the world around them. When Joshua became the leader of the children of Israel and led them across the Jordan River, the Lord instructed him on one way to begin the formation of that positive milieu.

## CIRCLES OF STONES

At the crossing, Joshua split the river so the children of Israel could cross on dry land, just as Moses had done with the Red Sea. When they crossed, one man from each tribe was to carry a stone from the riverbed and deposit it on the other side. There was a reason for the deliberate establishment of this memorial marker. Joshua explained its significance to the people: "This may be a sign among you. . . . and these stones shall be for a memorial unto the children of Israel for ever. . . . When your children shall ask their fathers in time to come, saying, What mean these stones? Then ye shall let your children know, saying, Israel came over this Jordan on dry land. For the Lord your God dried up the waters of Jordan from before *you*, until ye were passed over, as the Lord your God did to the Red sea, which he dried up from before *us*, until we were gone over" (Joshua 4:6-7, 21-23; emphasis added).

For generations into the future, the circle of stones placed by Joshua would elicit questions from curious children and thus give their parents the opportunity to tell the story of the miraculous crossing. The Lord knew the natural curiosity of the young and tapped into it for positive results. We all know that the teaching environment is better when questions are coming from the child instead of being offered by the parent. In the case of Joshua, a specific purpose was attached to the stones resting by the Jordan River. The telling of the story was to assure the inquisitive children that what the Lord did in the past he would continue to do. What he did for the parents he would do for the children. He will do for "you" what he did for "us." That would continue through the succeeding generations.

The celebration of the Passover was given to afford parents the opportunity at least once a year to tell the miraculous story of the Exodus to their offspring. Numerous times in his instructions to Moses, the Lord emphasized this aspect of the feast: "And it shall come to pass, when your children shall say unto you, What mean ye by this service? That ye shall say, It is the sacrifice of the Lord's passover, who passed over the houses of the children of Israel in Egypt" (Exodus 12:26–27). Later when speaking of the unleavened bread, the Lord instructed: "And thou shalt shew thy son in that day, saying, This is done because of that which the Lord did unto me when I came forth out of Egypt. . . . [And] when thy son asketh thee in time to come, saying, What is this? that thou shalt say unto him, By strength of hand the Lord brought us out from Egypt, from the house of bondage" (Exodus 13:8, 14). How often do we think of ordinances, holidays, or traditions as opportunities to teach curious children profound spiritual truths? These all can be circles of stones!

It is still desirable and necessary for us to make our own circle of stones, to create the environment, the memorials, which will bring questions and provide an opportunity to teach. We get some wonderful help in this area. A trip along the Church history trail, for example, visiting Palmyra or Nauvoo is a modern circle of stones provided for us by painstaking restoration projects supported by the Church. The pictures on our walls can become a circle of stones inviting a child to ask questions or a parent to relate stories of spiritual significance.

Perhaps one of the most influential circles of stones we can offer a child is in the name we choose to give him or her. Let us give them names to live up to. We learn of this in the book of Helaman. Two of the finest men presented to us are the brothers Nephi and Lehi. They converted the Lamanite nation in the midst of a great war and thus ended centuries of racial strife. We are given the words of their father, Helaman, when he named them at birth. "I have given unto you the names of our first parents who came out of the land of Jerusalem; and this I have done that when you remember your names ye may remember them; and when ye remember them ye may remember their works; and when ye remember their works ye may know how that it is said, and also written, that they were good. Therefore, my sons, I would that ye should do that which is good, that it may be said of you, and also written, even as it has been said and written of them" (Helaman 5:6–7).

A name to live up to may be the most significant memorial, the most permanent circle of stones, with which we can endow our children. Names can come from personalities in the scriptures, grandparents, ancestors, or prominent men or women in history who left a positive mark. The meaning of a child's name can also be a strong motivator. It is desirable for names to be more consequential than simply sounding good. Let them have a memorial nature attached to them so that every time a child thinks of her name, the person for whom she was named will come to mind. Because most of us give our children a first and a middle name, we have two opportunities to instill a potent level of inspiration.

For my grandparents' fiftieth wedding anniversary, my mother asked her parents to tell their life stories and those of their parents and grandparents. She obtained an old tape recorder and sat down with them each evening, encouraging the telling of memories and anecdotes from the past. I was a young boy, but I idolized my grandfather. My mother would put me to bed (so the house would be quiet) and begin the taping sessions. I remember crawling out of bed, opening my door a crack, placing my ear in the opening, and listening to marvelous stories about my ancestors. When she was finished, Mother typed the stories and gave me a copy. I read and reread that book until it was dog-eared, and when my grandparents visited, I would ask my grandfather to tell some of the stories to me. My mother had created a circle of stones that had their desired effect. The possibilities can be limitless if we concentrate on the task and look for memorial stones in our world.

## "BRING UP YOUR CHILDREN IN LIGHT AND TRUTH"

In the Doctrine and Covenants, the Lord is explicit in his directions that we control the environment surrounding our children. In section 93 particular emphasis is placed on the fact that Jesus did not receive "the fulness [of light and truth] at the first, but received grace for grace; and he received not of the fulness at first, but continued from grace to grace, until he received a fulness; and thus he was called the Son of God, because he received not of the fulness at the first" (D&C 93:12–14).

It hardly needs saying that God sincerely desires us to understand that his Beloved Son developed over the years of his youth in acquiring light and truth. The point is then made that we are to follow that same path: "If you keep my commandments you shall receive of his fulness . . . ; therefore, I say unto you, you shall receive grace for grace" (D&C 93:20).

What is the starting point for this continual growth toward the Father and the reception of his glory? It is ideal if it begins early, so the Lord offers us practical application of the doctrine of growing from grace to grace: "I have commanded you to bring up your children in light and truth" (D&C 93:40). The Lord then chastens Frederick G. Williams, Sidney Rigdon, Joseph Smith, and Newel K. Whitney for their failure to exert their first and best efforts to this necessity. Children are to be raised in an environment of light and truth. They are to begin the process of moving from grace to grace in an atmosphere of light. They are not to move from darkness to light but to commence in a state of grace. We are to give them a head start.

## THE SPIRITUAL MAGNET

In an earlier section of the Doctrine and Covenants we learn something about the nature of light and truth which should provide hope and encouragement for all parents. "For intelligence cleaveth unto intelligence; wisdom receiveth wisdom; truth embraceth truth; virtue loveth virtue; light cleaveth unto light" (D&C 88:40). The verbs in this passage are wonderful!

In section 93 the Lord indicates that "man was also in the beginning with God. Intelligence, or the light of truth, was not created or made. . . . Man is spirit. . . . Light and truth forsake that evil one" (D&C 93:29, 33, 37). As the saying goes, "Like attracts like." Because our children are, in their essential core, beings of intelligence, light, truth, and spirit, it is natural for them to cleave to, embrace, receive, and love light and goodness. True, they must learn to conquer the "natural man," but that conquest will be much easier if they are brought up in "light and truth." They have a spiritual magnet within them, which indeed is part of their very essence. It will pull intelligence into them. A parent's job is to surround the child with goodness, virtue, wisdom, truth, and light, to place in close proximity these things that they might be drawn into the soul.

Yes, we also live in a Canaanite world where there is precious little in broader society that supports our value system, but our children, beings of light and intelligence themselves, will naturally gravitate towards goodness, truth, mercy, and intelligence if we will provide that environment. We can be assured that in spite of the tremendous pull of worldly things, goodness and intelligence are stronger. Light always chases away darkness; darkness cannot overcome even a candle's worth of light. Darkness is the absence of light, not the extinguisher of it. To this Abinadi testified when he spoke of the Savior's light to the corrupt judges of King Noah's court: "He is the light and the life of the world; yea, a light that is endless, that can never be darkened" (Mosiah 16:9).

## MY FATHERS TURNED FROM THEIR RIGHTEOUSNESS

There is a very comforting thought in the knowledge that our children come from a premortal world of light and truth. They do bring certain dispositions with them that can be as powerful as the environment that surrounds them, if that setting is negative. I mention this because I have had numerous conversations with parents whose spouses do not share their convictions, either because they are not members of the Church or for other reasons. Sometimes there has been a divorce, with the believing parent sharing custody with a former spouse whose standards or values are dissimilar. Sometimes it is a relative, a sibling, a grandparent, an aunt, or an uncle who causes the anxiety. These wonderful mothers or fathers are concerned about conflicting messages being projected into their children's lives. A negative, disapproving, unconstructive, compromising, or even harmful situation need not be the deciding factor. The natural goodness of a child often rises above the most debilitating of surroundings and influences—even those from family members. They need not gravitate toward the easier, less spiritual, or more worldly path. In light of this, it is helpful to remember the example of Abraham.

We know something about the goodness Abraham brought to earth when he was born. In one of the most well-known verses in Latter-day Saint scripture we read of "the intelligences that were organized before the world was; and among all these there were many of the noble and great ones; and God saw these souls that they were good" (Abraham 3:22). We generally think of this goodness only in terms of future prophets or validation for our belief in a premortal world, but if applied to our situation, it can inspire confidence.

Abraham's nobility, created and mastered and refined in a life before birth, was superior to the horrible setting into which he was sent. As a young man, his internal goodness searched for something better than his own parents showed him. He discovered "there was greater happiness and peace and rest for me," and accordingly, "sought for the blessings of the fathers [the early great patriarchs]. . . . My fathers, having turned from their righteousness, and from the holy commandments which the Lord their God had given unto them, unto the worshipping of the gods of the heathen" (Abraham 1:2, 5). This pagan worship eventually led to the placing of Abraham himself as a sacrificial victim upon the heathen altars, and that by his own family. Yet Abraham turned out to be one of the noblest souls in scriptural history, the father of the faithful, and an example for all mankind. His premortal decency blazed through and overwhelmed the darkness of the world of his earthly family.

Sometimes we need to trust the innate integrity our children bring with them, and then do our utmost to provide a supportive environment within the limits that we can control. This is not always easy because we cannot see our children in their premortal lives and know the strength they can convey. Trusting our children's integrity can have a calming effect, leaving us more open to spiritual whisperings which will guide us as we face the day-to-day challenges of raising our children in a divided environment.

## HELPING THE SEEDLINGS TO GROW

Another compelling idea found in Doctrine and Covenants 93 is helpful for all mothers and fathers to consider, both as it relates to themselves and to their children. Three times we are told in this section that Jesus, the supreme example, did not obtain a fulness of light, truth, and glory all at once. He grew from grace to grace, from one level of righteousness to another. With each added piece of knowledge, he acted upon it correctly and matured in goodness. A close examination of this section seems to indicate that Jesus did not receive "a fulness of the glory of the Father" (v. 16) until his baptism at the hands of John in the Jordan River. At that time he was thirty years old. We must be patient with ourselves as we follow the Son's example, and we must be patient with our children.

A wonderful parable told by Mencius, the Chinese philosopher mentioned earlier, illustrates this point. "You must not be like the man from Sung," Mencius cautions. "There was a man from Sung who pulled at his seedlings because he was worried about their failure to grow. Having done so, he went on his way home, not realizing what he had done. 'I'm worn out today,' he said to his family. 'I have been helping the seedlings to grow.' His son rushed out to take a look and there the seedlings were, all shriveled up. There are very few in the world who can resist the urge to help their seedlings to grow. There are some who leave the seedlings unattended, thinking that nothing they do will be of any use. They are the people who do not even bother to weed. There are others who help the seedlings grow. They are the people who pull at them. Not only do they fail to help them, but they do the seedlings positive harm."[1]

We can push our children too fast in our anxiety about their development, whether spiritual, social, mental, or physical. As the man in the Savior's parable discovered, if you "cast seed into the ground; and should sleep, and rise night and day, and the seed should spring and grow up, he knoweth not how. For the earth bringeth forth fruit of herself; first the blade, then the ear, after that the full corn in the ear" (Mark 4:26–28). The good seed of our Father in Heaven's children will grow. Our job is to prepare and enrich the soil. Remember that in the parable of the sower, even the good soil produced at various rates of thirty, sixty, and a hundredfold. Is it not possible that those who one year were thirtyfold could become a hundredfold in time? Does not the parable suggest such an interpretation?

Mencius himself was the offspring of a wise mother who knew the importance of placing her son in an environment conducive to his development. Her house was located next to a graveyard, and she watched her son play at grave digging. "This is no place for my child," she thought, and she moved next to a market. There Mencius played at hawking goods. Again, his mother thought, "This is no place for my son." She then moved next to a Confucian school. There her son learned to think along Confucian lines. He played at scholarship and study. "This is truly a place for my son!"[2] And there she stayed. Her decision produced one of the greatest philosophers in Chinese history.

## "WHY HAVE YE DONE THIS?"

The importance of environment is never more clearly set forth than in the book of Judges. The generation of Israelites who entered the land of Canaan under Joshua had been tested and tried in the fire of their forty-year wandering in the wilderness. They were instructed by the Lord not to make any "league with the inhabitants of this land" (Judges 2:2). They were to drive them out of the land, but this was a difficult task, and it was easier to make treaties and force them to pay tribute. The first chapter of Judges is a fairly detailed list of the cities, areas, and tribes of the Canaanites the Israelites failed to remove. "Ye have not obeyed my voice: why have ye done this?" the Lord asks. He then tells them how foolish they have been in failing to secure a territory from which they had removed the idolatry and vicious worldly practices of Canaan. "They shall be as thorns in your sides, and their gods shall be a snare unto you" (Judges 2:2–3).

Interestingly, problems did not arise during the first generation. We are specifically told that "the people served the Lord all the days of Joshua, and all the days of the elders that outlived Joshua." Their wilderness training was sufficient to inoculate them against the immoralities and temptations of Canaan. It was not until "there arose another generation after them, which knew not the Lord," that the difficulties commenced. "They forsook the Lord God of their fathers, . . . and followed other gods, of the gods of the people that were round about them. . . . They turned quickly out of the way which their fathers walked in." Morals continued to decline with each succeeding generation. "They returned, and corrupted themselves more than their fathers" (Judges 2:7, 10, 12, 17, 19).

What might have been the history of Israel had that first generation created the environment commanded by the Lord? They followed many of the commandments, were a righteous people themselves, but they bequeathed to their children and grandchildren a world filled with temptation. As parents we must do our best to follow all the counsels of the Lord, for the very counsel or commandment we compromise may be the critical one for the next generation.

## MORAL GRAVITY

The first generation in Canaan failed to understand the principle of moral gravity. When two people are put together, one with a higher standard of behavior than the other, it is always desired that the higher will pull the lower up to their level, but that effort must be much greater because it is working against moral gravity. As we know, it is always easier to walk downhill than to climb uphill. That principle is equally true in spiritual and ethical matters. It is much less demanding for the higher to descend to the lower. We often see this in our children's choice of friends, but it can be true on a much broader scale, as we see in Judges. This theme is underscored as it is repeated again and again throughout the Old Testament whenever the children of Israel are drawn into the pagan practices associated with the worship of Baal. As children become more and more responsible for their own associations, it is helpful for them to have a good understanding of the pull of moral gravity so that they may make wise decisions regarding friends and environments. In spite of all their good intentions and perceived strengths, lifting a friend to a higher plateau may quickly be reversed, often without their even perceiving the change.

In 2 Chronicles a righteous but unwise king of Jerusalem named Jehoshaphat desired to heal the breach between the ten northern tribes and his own tribe of Judah, who were frequently engaged in civil war. He arranged a marriage with his son Jehoram to Athaliah, the daughter of Ahab and Jezebel, who were the unrighteous monarchs of the northern kingdom of Israel. Jehoshaphat arranged the marriage for the most sincere and righteous of reasons, but it turned into disaster, as Jehoram "walked in the way of the kings of Israel, like as did the house of Ahab: for he had the daughter of Ahab to wife: and he wrought that which was evil in the eyes of the Lord" (2 Chronicles 21:6). Among his evil deeds was the slaughter of his brothers. And the damage did not stop with Jehoram. When he died, his son followed in his wicked ways, "for his mother was his counsellor to do wickedly. Wherefore he did evil in the sight of the Lord like the house of Ahab: for they were his counsellors after the death of his father to his destruction" (2 Chronicles 22:3-4). Unfortunately we see this pattern far too often and in a circle whose arc encompasses so very many people.

Moral gravity also resists constructive change (or repentance), both personal and societal. When our behavior does not match our more elevated belief system, we become very uncomfortable. We feel the pangs of conscience. There are two ways to rectify the pain. We can raise our performance to match that of our ethics, or we can adapt our morals to the level of our conduct. It is obvious which requires the least amount of energy and therefore is the more common solution. We see this played out on the national, world, and religious stages of the world. Scriptural emphasis and warnings against the pull of moral gravity are strong. We provide our children with a sound defense if we teach them how moral gravity most frequently functions. We will be wiser parents if we understand how moral gravity works through generations in the legacies we create or allow.

In a nutshell, then, our challenge as parents can be simply

stated: Moral gravity works against us, while the spiritual magnet within each child works for us. If we surround our children with goodness, their core nature becomes an ally; if, however, they are encircled by negatives, the downward pull of moral gravity becomes an enemy. Our parental challenge becomes greater as society continues to decay and slip into ethical decline and relativism, but the restored gospel gives us more than an ample, offsetting hope.

## WEAKENING THE FENCES

As a boy I used to fix fence on my uncle's ranch. It was hard, dirty work and my least favorite job. We had to ride up and down the barbed wire fences, resetting posts and tightening the wires. The reason we were constantly fixing the fences was the cattle tended to eat the grass along the fence line. Once they had eaten all the grass on their side of the fence, the cattle would stick their heads through the wires or over the top of the fence to eat what was on the other side. In time, this constant straining against the wires and posts destroyed the fence.

The Lord has built some sturdy fences to protect his children. There is plenty of good green grass within those boundaries he has set, but often we strain at the limits of his standards. Parents may not stray outside those limits, but sometimes they strain against them, living the gospel on the edge. This may be true of certain forms of entertainment, fashions, lifestyles, Sabbath activities, or material possessions.

I noticed while herding the cattle that more often than not the adult cows did not go through the holes in the fence, but the calves did. We had to watch them. They were good at escaping through holes in the fence but not at recrossing the same downed fence line to return to their mothers and the herd.

If we are not watchful, we may weaken spiritual or moral fences, resulting in our children straying. One generation's exception often becomes the next generation's rule. In time this spiritual erosion takes its toll. If the cows had stayed in the center of the meadow, few calves would have ever been lost.

## "I CAN JUDGE"

When the Lord was communing with Moses before the deliverance of the Israelites from Egypt, he showed Moses his glory, which included his creations. Shortly thereafter, Satan appeared, tempting Moses to worship him, but Moses knew the difference between the two. "Blessed be the name of my God," Moses said, "for his Spirit hath not altogether withdrawn from me, or else where is thy glory, for it is darkness unto me? And I can judge between thee and God" (Moses 1:15). Later, when Satan persisted in his temptations, Moses once again certified that he knew the difference between the two, having first seen the glory of God. "His glory has been upon me, wherefore I can judge between him and thee. Depart hence, Satan" (Moses 1:18).

We are here in mortality to learn to distinguish between good and evil. Mothers and fathers are to help their inexperienced children forge the foundation for choosing between the two. Is that not the true definition of godhood? A god always knows the difference between good and evil and then acts on that knowledge by always choosing the good.

This is most effectively accomplished by presenting good things first, as the Lord did with Moses, so our children have a standard by which they can judge everything else. We know darkness because we have seen light. We know bitter because we have tasted the sweet. If I wish my child to watch only the best movies, I must introduce her to them so she can tell the difference between edifying presentations and those which simply appeal to her most ignoble and base instincts. If I want my child to listen to uplifting, proper music, he must hear it in our home, so he can tell the difference when the crass music of the world blares into his earphones. If I desire that my children read great literature, I must acquaint them with it, so they have a standard by which to judge.

Good taste in these types of things is created in the home, by the art which decorates our walls and the topics discussed at the dinner table. They must see the glory first, and then they are armed for the darkness which will surely come. Then they will say, "I can judge." A few examples may be illustrative.

## GREEK GRACE AND OSCAR WILDE

When I was in elementary school, my mother brought home an antique Greek marble statue of a beautiful woman drinking delicately from a small bowl. She was about eighteen inches tall and mounted on a polished granite base. I don't know how much it cost, but on an elementary schoolteacher's salary, I'm sure there was some sacrifice involved in it. In the classical Greek style she was nude, but I never saw her as a sensual object. She was grace in stone, and she awoke in me a longing for all that was beautiful, for all that was Greek. I read their myths, studied their history, wondered at their architecture, and appreciated their literature. I continued to love the Greek world, and that world soon spread to include a fascination for Rome and in time the Renaissance.

My life was enriched by contact with an element of loveliness which I saw every day. As I grew older I could not help but compare all art with the feeling of reverent awe and appreciation for the dignity of humankind I received every time I walked in the house and saw the beautiful statue resting in her accustomed place on top of the piano. In time she became an object of mirth and good-hearted fun for the youth of the stake, who loved to sew clothes for Sister Wilcox's "naked lady," but she continued to represent all that was graceful and lovely to me. When Mother sold the house in California and needed to simplify her belongings for a move to Utah, she asked me what I wanted. There was no hesitation—I chose the Greek statue. She now graces my own house, and I continue to receive that refined sense of charm and elegance she imparts. I do not think my mother had any idea what impact her purchase would produce, but she created an environment that paid long-term dividends in the life of her son.

My mother did a similar thing in the realm of literature by reading to my sisters and me the tales of Oscar Wilde. This was my first encounter with the world of "wisdom" one could "seek" in the "best books" (D&C 88:118). As with the marble statue, there was a quality in Wilde's writing that stirred things within me and created a taste for beauty and light in the written word. I have compared all stories to what I discovered and felt in Oscar Wilde. In time the desire to experience the lift I felt in reading Wilde led me to Dickens, Austen, Thoreau, and finally Shakespeare. We must certainly be mindful of the religious atmosphere with which we surround our sons and daughters, and we must keep in mind other considerations as well. I am grateful that I had a mother who introduced into my life a measure of goodness which produced a hunger to seek for the nobler things brought forth by the mind and creative genius of man.

⌒

## CHAPTER ELEVEN

Chasten thy son while there is hope,
and let not thy soul spare for his crying. . . . Cease,
my son, to hear the instruction that causeth to err
from the words of knowledge.
*Proverbs 19:18, 27*

# Learning to Say No

## "HE RESTRAINED THEM NOT"

Ironically, one of the most difficult yet necessary qualities all leaders need to develop is the ability to sometimes say no to those they lead. Raising a child is leadership of the most intensely serious kind. Many times parents with their greater wisdom can see that their child's behavior or decisions will, either in the short or long term, bring undesirable consequences or fail to deliver desirable ones. Yet a parent does not wish to strain a relationship, disappoint a child, or worse, cause rebellion or alienation. These can be delicate situations requiring thought and tact. I know that in my own case it is often much easier just to give in, say okay, give permission, or compromise when my deepest convictions tell me the best thing is to stand firm. We want our children to love us. We want them to like us. A happy smile of relief on a child's face may be temptation enough to ignore the anxious worries that often follow a yes that should have been a no. These considerations become even more necessary when a child's behavior or desires have significant consequences not only for the child but sometimes for generations into the future.

In the first book of Samuel we are introduced to Eli, the high priest, and his two sons, Hophni and Phinehas. The two sons were placed in positions of trust at the tabernacle in Shiloh, but they "were sons of Belial [a derogatory term for a wicked man]; they knew not the Lord" (1 Samuel 2:12). Their disgraceful acts during their ministrations at the tabernacle were a scandal to all Israel and alienated many to the service of the Lord. Under these circumstances, it was Eli's duty as both high priest and father to restrain or remove them, but he did neither. Eli did make a feeble effort to motivate their reform, but it lacked teeth. "Why do ye such things?" he asked. "I hear of your evil dealings by all this people. Nay, my sons; for it is no good report that I hear: ye make the Lord's people to transgress. . . . Notwithstanding they hearkened not unto the voice of their father" (1 Samuel 2:23–24, 25).

Given ample time to correct his sons and failing, Eli was finally addressed by the Lord through the mouth of a messenger. "Wherefore . . . honourest thy sons against me . . . ?" (2 Samuel 2:29). During this time the boy Samuel was working at the temple. A revelation to Eli was sent through Samuel explaining why Eli and his descendants would be removed from the priestly office. "I have told him that I will judge his house for ever for the iniquity which he knoweth; because his sons made themselves vile, and he restrained them not" (1 Samuel 3:13).

Later, when his two sons took the ark of the covenant into battle, Eli did nothing, even though "his heart trembled for the ark of God" (1 Samuel 4:13). This was a time for courage and leadership, but trembling was all Eli could muster. The ark of the covenant was lost in the battle and though later it was miraculously returned to Israel, both Hophni and Phinehas were killed. When Eli heard the news of his sons' deaths and that the ark had been lost, he fell "from off the seat backward by the side of the gate" (1 Samuel 4:18), broke his neck, and died.

## GOLDEN CALVES AND KINGS

In a similar failure of leadership, Aaron foolishly made the golden calf for the children of Israel at their insistence while Moses tarried on Sinai. When Moses returned, he asked Aaron, "What did this people unto thee, that thou hast brought so great a sin upon them?"

Aaron's weak answer showed his inability to stand firm when courage, not compromise, was needed. "Thou knowest the people, that they are set on mischief" (Exodus 32:21, 22). When the young, the inexperienced, or the willful are set on misguided mischief, someone—most often their parents—must say no, even at the cost of incurring resentment and criticism.

King Benjamin instructed his people on the need to sometimes restrict the negative inclinations of a child, including behavior within the family. According to his counsel, parents had responsibilities beyond the physical needs of the child for food, shelter, and clothing. "And ye will not suffer your children that they go hungry, or naked; neither will ye suffer that they transgress the laws of God, and fight and quarrel one with another, and serve the devil, who is the master of sin. . . . But ye will teach them to walk in the ways of truth and soberness; ye will teach them to love one another, and to serve one another" (Mosiah 4:14–15).

Most of the book of Ether was included in the Book of Mormon to highlight the very principle we are examining. As Jared and Mahonri Moriancumer (the brother of Jared) neared the end of their lives, Moriancumer said to Jared, "Let us gather together our people that we may number them, that we may know of them what they will desire of us before we go down to our graves" (Ether 6:19). The answer they received was distressing. "It came to pass that the people desired of them that they should anoint one of their sons to be a king over them. And now behold, this was grievous unto them. And the brother of Jared said unto them: Surely this thing leadeth into captivity" (Ether 6:22–23). Their greater wisdom and experience with life and the corrupting influence of power told them this was a dangerous request. But at a time when they should have stood firm, one brother weakened, and the other deferred to his decision. "Jared said unto his brother: Suffer them that they may have a king" (Ether 6:24).

Though the first king chosen proved to be righteous, the long, sad history of the Jaredites begins within a few verses of Jared's fatal decision. We soon read of conflict, as father fights son and brother plots against brother in a never-ending grasp for power that eventually leads to the entire destruction of the Jaredite race. Nine chapters of scripture validate a moment's decision when a parent needed to stand firm, say no, and mean it. Even the Father, in the Garden of Eden after Adam and Eve had partaken of the fruit of the tree of knowledge of good and evil, placed cherubim and a flaming sword before the tree of life to prevent Adam and Eve from partaking of its fruit and bringing eternal consequences upon their heads.

President John F. Kennedy, while serving as a United States senator, wrote a book titled *Profiles in Courage*, wherein he related stories of valor manifested by past senators who went against their party or their constituents to support legislation they believed to be best for the nation. One such case was that of John Quincy Adams's support of President Thomas Jefferson's embargo of British goods during a period of tension between the two nations. Though extremely unpopular in Massachusetts, Adams's home district, he supported the embargo against the vicious opposition of critics. He believed he was committing political suicide, yet he continued with his support. At the time, he wrote the following eloquent statement of the principle we are now exploring: "Highly as I revered the authority of my constituents, and bitter as would have been the cup of resistance to their declared will . . . I would have defended their interests against their inclinations and incurred every possible addition to their resentment to save them from the vassalage of their own delusions."[1]

Parents must often do the same. If a child knows the parent's reasoning and perceives the opposition not to be arbitrary but the result of love and concern, he or she is more likely to accept the disappointment. There are no guarantees, of course, but a past relationship of trust, built over years, will do much to mitigate resentment or rebellion. In the case of the Jaredites, so great was their respect for Moriancumer that all of his sons refused the kingship and all but one of Jared's sons did likewise.

## PROTEST SOLEMNLY WITHOUT FORSAKING

There are balancing principles to consider also. It would be wonderful if we had a concrete rule to tell us when to say no and stick to it and when to pursue another course. The scriptures as a whole contain the proper balance if we know where to look. In 1 Samuel, the Israelites, like the Jaredites, demanded a king. Once again the request was deemed by Samuel and the Lord a dangerous and unwise decision, yet this time the Lord consented. In his consenting, however, we learn how best to respond to an unwise request when we fear alienation, rebellion, or dangerously damaging consequences to the ongoing relationship.

When Samuel presented the people's desire for a king to the Lord, the Lord responded by saying, "They have rejected me, that I should not reign over them. . . . Now therefore hearken unto their voice: howbeit yet protest solemnly unto them, and shew them the manner of the king that shall reign over them" (1 Samuel 8:7, 9).

The Lord does four things we can consider when faced with similar situations within the walls of our own homes. Three of them are in the passage from 1 Samuel. First, the Lord knew their desire was dangerous, but he honored their agency when he told Samuel to "hearken unto their voice." Depending on the age of the son or daughter, parents must take agency into consideration and honor it. Second, he "protest[ed] solemnly." Even though a child is given his agency, he needs to know the true feelings of the parent. The protest is given not in anger nor peevishness nor with resentment but *solemnly*. The word suggests the opposition is given sincerely, earnestly, seriously, gravely, fervently, even with a touch of sadness. Yet that sadness is not given with meanness or in a spirit of resignation that says to the child, "I guess you have to learn the hard way." It is given in kindness and concern. Third, the Lord explained to the Israelites the probable consequences of their actions. Moriancumer did the same with the Jaredites when he told them their desire would surely lead to captivity. In 1 Samuel, Samuel gives a detailed list of consequences if they move forward with their anointing of a king. The people failed to appreciate the seriousness of their position and continued to demand a king. Thus Saul was chosen.

Here we learn of the fourth and final—and, I believe, most important—step a parent may need to take when a child will not take a simple or a persuasive no for an answer. The Lord was not vindictive. He chose the best man he could as king: "Saul, a choice young man, and a goodly: and there was not among the children of Israel a goodlier person than he" (1 Samuel 9:2). When Saul was presented to the people, Samuel reiterated his earlier solemn protest and then added, "Fear not. . . . For the Lord will not forsake his people. . . . As for me,

God forbid that I should [cease] to pray for you: but I will teach you the good and the right way: Only fear the Lord . . . for consider how great things he hath done for you" (1 Samuel 12:20, 22–24).

The fourth and final step, then, is not to forsake the child, either literally or emotionally, but to continue to pray for him or her and teach the good and right way, hoping that past things that have been done for the child will continue to weigh on his or her mind. The relationship must not be permanently damaged if it is avoidable. I think the Lord and Samuel were trying to lessen the injury that would result from the people's foolishness in rejecting the wiser counsel. Yet they tried to maintain the relationship and the opportunity to give future guidance.

In review, then, here are the steps the Lord and Samuel used with their misdirected people's desires:

1. Honor their agency.
2. Protest solemnly.
3. Explain the probable consequences.
4. Do not forsake them, but continue to pray for them and teach them.

This pattern can minimize the consequences of a child's mistaken choices.

The book of Proverbs often speaks of the necessity of children listening to their parent's counsel. This begins as early as the first chapter: "My son, hear the instruction of thy father, and forsake not the law of thy mother: For they shall be an ornament of grace unto thy head, and chains about thy neck" (Proverbs 1:8–9). This is beautiful imagery. We want our counsel to grace and adorn our children, like jewels. They may not always see it that way, however. In those cases the last thing we want is for them to remove the "ornament of grace" or the chain, discard it, and walk away. There is always hope if they keep that counsel about them, even if only in their purse or pocket.

## CHAPTER TWELVE

And he arose, and came to his father.
But when he was yet a great way off, his father saw
him, and had compassion, and ran, and fell
on his neck, and kissed him.
*Luke 15:20*

# Helping the Struggling and the Wayward

## PARENTAL SUCCESS? PARENTAL FAILURE?

It is difficult to refrain from measuring our abilities as a parent by the character of our children. In our world we are so accustomed to judge success by the outcome that it is next to impossible not to do the same thing when raising a family, both as we assess our own efforts and those of people we know. We become comparative, doing justice neither to ourselves nor to others. If our children turn out well, it may be that we were tremendous parents, making few mistakes and guiding them in a wise and patient way, but it may be that we received spirits from the Lord who would have flourished in almost any home. Remember, Abraham came from a horrible home, yet few in history were more devoted and righteous.

If our children struggle or are wayward and our hearts are pained as we watch their choices, it may be that we have made serious mistakes in raising them and, with due respect to their own agency, we may bear a significant part of the blame in the formation of their characters. It is equally possible, however, that no parents could have done a finer job, that those spirits' only real hope of surviving their earthly existence in a state of virtue and decency was to be placed in our home, where at least they would have a righteously supportive setting to curb their more rebellious or independent natures. We must be careful, in assessing our parental efforts, to leave a wide latitude of possibilities. We want neither unholy pride nor unfounded guilt. Gratitude for their goodness or hope in their amendment are much better emotions to cultivate when pondering our children.

While a member of the Quorum of the Twelve, President Howard W. Hunter taught that "a successful parent is one who has loved, one who has sacrificed, and one who has cared for, taught, and ministered to the needs of a child. If you have done all of these and your child is still wayward or troublesome or worldly, it could well be that you are, nevertheless, a successful parent. Perhaps there are children who have come into the world that would challenge any set of parents under any set of circumstances. Likewise, perhaps there are others who would bless the lives of, and be a joy to, almost any father or mother."[1]

We must also remind ourselves that children change. The prodigal son did return and receive his father's ring. Alma the Younger and the sons of Mosiah were "born again" (Alma 7:14). The persecuting Saul became the preaching Apostle Paul. Esau, after experiencing apathy and misdirected anger, in time received his brother Jacob with a forgiving embrace.

My grandfather lived into his nineties. I once asked him when I was a little boy, "Grandpa, how come you're so old?" He laughed and answered, "Well, Mike, God can make a good man out of some people in forty or fifty years, but your grandpa was a hard nut to crack, and it'll take the Lord eighty or ninety years to do the job with me." Some of us may have been given children that are "hard nuts to crack." Remember, in the parable of the wheat and tares, the Lord cautioned against removing the tares too early because some of the wheat might also be rooted out. What appears in an early stage of life to be a tare may in time prove to have always been wheat.

This is not to say that our children come from heaven already formed and the outcome is practically set. It simply means we must leave most of the judging to him who knows all the possibilities and views all of life through a divine lens, one who sees the premortal, the mortal, and the postmortal in a manner we cannot.

## ALMA'S PATTERN OF CORRECTION

In the meantime, what can we do if we need to correct a struggling child, reclaim the errant, calm the rebellious, or go after the lost? Let us return to those rich chapters in the Book of Mormon where Alma the Younger speaks with each of his children separately. One of them, Corianton, is struggling with his faith as well as having hamstrung his father's efforts with the Zoramites by going "into the land of Siron . . . after the harlot Isabel" (Alma 39:3).

I sense a pattern in Alma's words to his son in Alma 39. It consists of four parts that can provide a beginning for a parent. They need to be adapted to suit each individual situation and personality, but they are remarkably insightful. They are given in a tone of patience and love and are nonconfrontational and supportive.

*First*—Show them where they have gone wrong, are mistaken, or have brought themselves to their present situation. Alma does this in the following phrases he said to Corianton: "Thou didst not give so much heed unto my words. . . . Thou didst go on unto boasting in thy strength and thy wisdom. . . . Thou didst forsake the ministry, and did go over into the land of Siron. . . . She did steal away the hearts of many; but this was no excuse for thee, my son" (Alma 39:2-4).

Corianton's problems arose from giving not "so much" heed to counsel (which suggests he did give some heed); thinking he was stronger and wiser than he was (a common assumption of us all, but particularly the young); ceasing to be engaged in good things (usually the beginning of spiritual problems); finding himself in the wrong environment (the logical next step); and excusing actions because of what others were doing, (the most frequent rationalization for compromised behavior). These are all standard problems, especially for the young.

*Second*—Explain the short- and long-term consequences of their conduct. Alma made clear to his son that his deeds brought "great iniquity . . . upon the Zoramites; for when they saw your conduct they would not believe in my words" (Alma 39:11). He also suggested that behavior such as Corianton's would "harrow up your soul" and that Corianton needed to "return unto them [the Zoramites], and acknowledge your faults" (Alma 39: 7, 13).

Long-term consequences may or may not come to pass. Those depend upon the individual and his or her willingness to redirect their lives. "Ye cannot hide your crimes from God; and except ye repent they will stand as a testimony against you at the last day. . . . Except ye do this ye can in nowise inherit the kingdom of God" (Alma 39:8-9). Long-term consequences tend to be serious, and it is important they are not projected in a threatening manner. No one is ever ultimately condemned for their sins. They are condemned because they refuse to leave them. To utilize a sports metaphor, there is always a second half to life, in which we can correct errors and ultimately win the victory. Often short-term consequences, when faced, prevent the long-term, usually more serious ones, from happening at all.

When I was in elementary school, baseball was the passion of America. We all had our favorite teams and players, and most of us collected baseball cards. For a nickel you could buy five cards and a piece of bubble gum. I did chores for baseball card money, and I collected pop bottles. You received two cents for a small bottle and five cents for a large one. I scoured the fields and streets for discarded bottles. One day, I happened to see in a neighbor's garage a veritable fortune in pop bottles. The temptation was too great, and because no one was home, I helped myself. I soon discovered that most people in the neighborhood stored pop bottles in their garage. It was too easy. I hoarded them all in a fort I had built in the rafters of our garage.

All was well until my mother saw a glint of glass and asked what I had up there. "Pop bottles," I answered.

Then came the question I dreaded: "Where did you get so many?"

I never could lie to my mother, and the truth was out. My short-term consequence was an invitation by my mother to return the bottles with an apology, just as Alma instructed his son to return to the Zoramites to acknowledge his faults. I loaded up my wagon and pulled it up and down the street, knocking on doors and asking everyone if they remembered how many bottles they had had because I was returning them. Everyone was kind to me, and I'm sure they smiled inwardly, but I never forgot it. I determined I would not suffer that kind of humiliation and embarrassment again.

I contrast this memory with one concerning a close friend of mine. During high school he was suspended for a serious infraction of school rules involving alcohol. His parents were irate with the principal and demanded the school drop the punishment. They were influential, the school authorities backed down, and he was returned to school the next day. This was a pattern with which I was familiar in his relationship with his parents. His life deteriorated until, in time, he was arrested for selling drugs. There is a natural desire in parents to protect their children from undesirable consequences. This we all understand; however, more painful, long-term results may be avoided if children face the short-term effects of their decisions. We must be careful and wise so that we do not, in the name of love, refrain from taking away outcomes that are needed for character growth.

*Third*—Teach them how to avoid problems in the future. Arm them against repeated temptation. Alma begins this step by stressing the seriousness of Corianton's offenses. "Know ye not, my son, that these things are an abomination in the sight of the Lord. . . . I would to God that ye had not been guilty of so great a crime" (Alma 39:5, 7). He also indicates the need for his son to control his passions, which depends almost entirely upon himself. "Go no more after the lusts of your eyes, but cross yourself in all these things. . . . Oh, remember, and take it upon you, and cross yourself in these things" (Alma 39:9). Alma gives additional preventative advice. "Counsel with your elder brothers in your undertakings. . . . Turn to the Lord with all your mind, might, and strength. . . . Seek not after riches nor the vain things of this world" (Alma 39:10, 13-14). Alma focuses on the broader lifestyle that fosters immoral behavior. Doing well is generally the best way to prevent doing ill. "If thou doest well," the Lord told Cain, "thou shalt be accepted. And if thou doest not well, sin lieth at the door" (Moses 5:23).

I have an interesting oak tree in my backyard. In the fall the leaves all die, but they do not fall off. At first this distressed me, because I wanted to be finished with the leaf raking once and for all. I shook the tree to make the leaves fall, all to no avail. Even knocking the branches with a rake failed to dislodge the stubborn leaves. I finally had to give up and just allow the ugly brown leaves to remain on the tree for the winter. In the spring, however, as the new leaves emerged, the old dry ones fell off easily, replaced by the growing life. So it is with bad habits or sin. It might be a better plan to encourage a child to initiate good behavior instead of only pressing for the removal of old habits. The old passes away more easily with the coming of the new.

*Fourth*—End with forgiveness and hope. Alma's speech was very plain—perhaps too plain for some today—but after speaking so directly to Corianton, he shifted his attention to the sacrifice of the Savior in order to instill hope. "And now, my son, I would say somewhat unto you concerning the coming of Christ. Behold, I say unto you, that it is he that surely shall come to take away the sins of the world. . . . You marvel why these things should be known so long beforehand. Behold, I say unto you, is not a soul at this time as precious unto God as a soul will be at the time of his coming?" (Alma 39:15, 17). Alma then spent considerable time explaining the doctrines of the Atonement, ending with these beautiful words: "Let the justice of God, and his mercy, and his long-suffering have full sway in your heart" (Alma 42:30). His concluding words express his continued confidence in his son and a renewal of Corianton's call. "And now, O my son, ye are called of God to preach the word unto this people" (Alma 42:31).

## CORRECT EARLY WITH TRUTH

This ending with hope, love, confidence, and forgiveness is strongly taught in the Doctrine and Covenants. There are times when "reproving betimes with sharpness" is necessary (D&C 121:43). More plainly stated, this phrase means to *correct* (reprove) *early* (betimes)—before the problem gets too big—*with truth* (sharpness).

We do not reprove with anger. Lehi explained this beyond question when talking to Laman and Lemuel about Nephi's "sharpness." "Ye say that he hath used sharpness; ye say that he hath been angry with you; but behold, his sharpness was the sharpness of the power of the word of God, which was in him; and that which ye call anger was the truth" (2 Nephi 1:26). After the correction is given, however, the Lord tells us, we must "[show] forth afterwards an increase of love toward him whom thou hast reproved, lest he esteem thee to be his enemy; that he may know that thy faithfulness is stronger than the cords of death" (D&C 121:43–44). Alma is a prime example of these teachings.

## "I PERCEIVE"

Alma shows us another quality in the chapters dealing with his son. Corianton has many questions about the doctrines of the gospel. He has apparently used these doubts and uncertainties as excuses for his behavior. Doubt and uncertainty are often used as a barrier to hide behind when living the gospel is difficult, unaccomplished, or undesirable. "If I'm not convinced or sure it is true, I don't have to live it," is the reasoning.

At the beginning of each of the three doctrinal chapters containing Alma's teachings, we find a discerning of Corianton's mind by his father. "*I perceive* that thy mind is worried" (Alma 40:1; emphasis added). "*I perceive* that thy mind has been worried also concerning this thing. But behold, I will explain it unto thee" (Alma 41:1; emphasis added). "And now, my son, *I perceive* there is somewhat more which doth worry your mind, which ye cannot understand. . . . I will explain this thing unto thee" (Alma 42:1–2; emphasis added).

It is critical that mothers and fathers listen to the unspoken thoughts of their children. One must be in tune with the Spirit in order to do this, but the rewards are great. There is no indication that Corianton voiced his worries, but Alma perceived them and set his son's mind at rest. Alma did not just pour out his counsel; he watched his son's face, knew some of his past concerns, listened to his son's mind, and with the help of the Spirit directed his words where they could do the most good. Such perceptive, sensitive listening is a talent most needful and yet one hard to acquire, especially if we are most concerned with controlling the conversation by emptying our own thoughts upon our child instead of receiving from our child his or her real and deep concerns.

We do know that Alma was successful with his son. In chapter 63 of Alma, Shiblon, who had charge of the sacred records, desired to pass them on to his younger brother, Corianton. This he could not do, however, for Corianton had gone into the land northward. "Therefore it became expedient for Shiblon to confer those sacred things, before his death, upon the son of Helaman" (Alma 63:10–11).

## THERE ARE NO PERFECT PARENTS

Before leaving our discussion of Alma's charge to his son Corianton, it might be helpful to ponder one more item. Parents are not perfect—even the best ones make mistakes when dealing with their children. I do not wish to be controversial or to judge Alma's parenting, as I have learned much from him. Yet he does say something to Corianton that students in my classes have pointed out to me several times. Alma's introductory words to his wayward son are as follows: "I have somewhat more to say unto thee than what I said unto thy brother; for behold, have ye not observed the steadiness of thy brother, his faithfulness, and his diligence in keeping the commandments of God? Behold, has he not set a good example for thee?" (Alma 39:1).

Sibling comparisons may be positive and inspiring, but few of us respond warmly to such an evaluation, especially when we are defensive and given to excuses, as it appears Corianton was at the commencement of his conversation with his father. Yet in spite of what some might consider a questionable beginning, the warmth, care, patience, and understanding of Alma prove to be a winning combination.

We all make mistakes with our sons and daughters. We are learning how to become parents as we teach our children how to become responsible contributing adults. There must be forgiveness on both ends. We cannot expect mature perfection in our children, just as they must realize they cannot expect perfection in the parenting skills of their parents.

We have not done this before; just as we do when we are learning to ride a bicycle, we are bound to crash occasionally. I once said to my daughter when I had made a parental blunder—which she pointed out with some eagerness—that I was grateful for her help in making me a better parent. I hoped she would forgive me my frequent ineptitudes as she helped me learn how to be a better parent. In return, I would forgive her errors as she learned how to master earthly maturity with its spiritual and moral independence.

This understanding saved us from many hurt feelings, resentments, and disappointed expectations. I like to teasingly point out that she has turned out pretty well, so her parents must have done at least an adequate job.

## THE SAVIOR'S MANNER OF CORRECTION

There is another place in scripture where we can discern a pattern for encouraging improvement in behavior. We find this model in the book of Revelation, an epistle directed to the seven churches of Asia Minor. Each of these churches was facing problems, many of which were the result of their own aberrant conduct. Though the pattern is not consistent for all seven churches, it is typical and thus enlightening.

The Lord does three things with the churches. First, he finds something to praise. Having pointed out their good qualities, it is less threatening to them when he moves to the next area. Second, he chastens them for their irregularities. These he points out with plainness, leaving no doubt about his concerns. That disquiet centers on the people and their welfare, not some arbitrary slight to his dignity. Third, he promises them a glorious outcome if they can overcome their temptations and difficulties.

An examination of one of the churches will be sufficient as an example. To the Saints in Ephesus the Lord begins: "I know thy works, and thy labour, and thy patience, and how thou canst not bear them which are evil . . . and has borne, and hast patience, and for my name's sake hast laboured and hast not fainted." But all is not right in Ephesus, which the Lord then points out: "Nevertheless I have somewhat against thee, because thou hast left thy first love." They need to reexamine their priorities and place God first. Then the promise: "To him that overcometh will I give to eat of the tree of life, which is in the midst of the paradise of God" (Revelation 2:2-4, 7).

Though the pattern of praise/chastisement/promise is not the same for all seven cities, each one, without exception, receives a promise for overcoming. Likewise, no child is devoid of areas in his or her life which are worthy of adulation. We need to look for them, and remember that rewarding positive behavior often proves to be more effective than punishing negative actions. Depending on the circumstances, the child's maturity, or the seriousness of the offense, a combination of both Alma's and the Savior's pattern may prove the most valuable.

## "IN A PROPER AND AFFECTIONATE MANNER"

Joseph Smith made an observation that, although not immediately related to parenting, is nonetheless very relevant to our present topic. He was reflecting on the severe persecution he had endured after the First Vision. Notice the importance of the key words as they apply to correcting someone we feel is wrong or needs to change direction. This is what he wrote:

"Being of very tender years, and persecuted by those who *ought to have been my friends* and to have *treated me kindly,* and if they supposed me to be deluded to have endeavored in *a proper and affectionate manner* to have reclaimed me—I was left to all kinds of temptations . . . [and] frequently fell into many foolish errors and displayed the weakness of youth" (JS–H 1:28; emphasis added).

Because we all prefer, especially when we are wrong, to be treated in a friendly, kindly, proper, and affectionate manner, it is most necessary to do the same with others. Our own heart becomes the model for all other hearts. Above all, we do not leave the child to temptation, error, or weakness. This we saw in our discussion of 1 Samuel with the people's desire for a king and the Lord's response to their folly.

Once a child has changed, the parable of the prodigal son proves the most exemplary of a proper attitude for the parent. Though the son feels unworthy of his father ("I . . . am no more worthy to be called thy son"), the father runs to greet his return "when he was yet a great way off," bestowing an embrace and parental kiss. Then to the astonishment of the wayward son, the father dresses the returning son in his best robe, places his ring on his hand, thus sealing the family connection, puts shoes on his feet, and kills the fatted calf in a ceremony of welcome (see Luke 15:18–24).

I imagine the father did not mention to his son his sinful life. In the son's penitent return, that life was past, and all eyes needed to be toward the future. There is so much hope in that future.

## CHAPTER THIRTEEN

And that same sociality which exists among us here
will exist among us there, only it will be coupled
with eternal glory, which glory we do not now enjoy.
*Doctrine and Covenants 130:2*

# "And Minist'ring Angels, to Happify There"

## "O MY SON ABSALOM"

Sometimes, in spite of all our best and most loving efforts, a son or daughter refuses to respond, and parents feel one of the deepest heartaches of life. Lehi and Sariah felt it with Laman and Lemuel; Adam and Eve experienced it with Cain; Jacob knew it with a number of his sons, including Reuben, Levi, Simeon, and Judah; Samson's decision to marry a Philistine grieved his parents; and the Father's weeping in Moses 7 places this pain on a cosmic scale. Some parents, such as Alma the Elder and Mosiah, knew the distress of straying children but later the intense relief of their repentance and subsequent righteousness.

I can think of no father or mother who expressed this anguish so poignantly as did David at the death of Absalom. It is especially touching considering Absalom had rebelled against David, usurped his throne, despoiled his wives, and had earlier killed his half-brother

Amnon for violating his sister Tamar. There were enough reasons in David's heart to be tormented by the actions of his son.

While waiting for news of the battle his own men were fighting against his son in his behalf, David watched by the gate. When runners were seen approaching the city, David knew they carried the tidings of the day. To his anxious inquiry, "Is the young man Absalom safe?" the messenger answered, "The enemies of my lord the king, and all that rise against thee to do thee hurt, be as that young man is. And the king was much moved, and went up to the chamber over the gate, and wept: and as he went, thus he said, O my son Absalom, my son, my son Absalom! Would God I had died for thee, O Absalom, my son, my son!" (2 Samuel 18:32–33).

Surely part of that intense grief was not only due to the loss of his son's life but because he died in a state of deep rebellion and spiritual alienation.

## "ETERNAL SEALINGS"

Is there no comfort for this depth of suffering? I believe there is. We find it in the Doctrine and Covenants and in the power of the sealing ordinances of the temple. We have been assured that if the parents are faithful to their covenants, promises regarding their children are in store.

Elder Orson F. Whitney recalled that "the Prophet Joseph Smith declared—and he never taught a more comforting doctrine— that the eternal sealings of faithful parents and the divine promises made to them for valiant service in the Cause of Truth, would save not only themselves, but likewise their posterity. Though some of the sheep may wander, the eye of the Shepherd is upon them, and sooner or later they will feel the tentacles of Divine Providence reaching out after them and drawing them back to the fold. Either in this life or the life to come, they will return. They will have to pay their debt to justice; they will suffer for their sins; and may tread a thorny path; but if it leads them at last, like the penitent Prodigal, to a loving and forgiving Father's heart and home, the painful experience will not have been in vain. Pray for your careless and disobedient children; hold on to them with your faith. Hope on. Trust on, till you see the salvation of God."[1]

President Brigham Young made similar assurances. "Let the father and mother, who are members of this Church and Kingdom, take a righteous course, and strive with all their might never to do a wrong, but to do good all their lives; if they have one child or one hundred children, if they conduct themselves towards them as they should, binding them to the Lord by their faith and prayers, I care not where those children go, they are bound up to their parents by an everlasting tie, and no power of earth or hell can separate them from their parents in eternity; they will return again to the fountain from whence they sprang."[2]

## "TO HAPPIFY THERE"

I have talked to many parents with wandering children who are both comforted and confused by these statements. "Does our sealing in the temple and living a righteous life guarantee that one day our wayward children will return and be heirs of the celestial kingdom with us? What about the other scriptures that indicate each individual must live a valiant life?" Sometimes they quote the Doctrine and Covenants: "He who is not able to abide the law of a celestial kingdom cannot abide a celestial glory" (D&C 88:22).

Their questions are sometimes worded differently, but the parents' bewilderment is usually the same. They want to fully believe these lovely encouragements, which are full of hope, but they struggle with a concept that, unless they have read Elder Whitney's words carefully, could seem to contradict other scriptural truths.[3]

How can we integrate this comforting doctrine with the many scriptures that teach us that we will be judged by our own deeds, not the righteousness (or unrighteousness) of our parents? In asserting one truth we cannot do injury to other truths. All must fit like the spokes of a wheel into its hub. Complete answers may not be forthcoming with our limited understanding, but some insight may still be gained with a little thought. The rest we will leave in the hands and heart of a merciful Father in Heaven.

Perhaps there is an answer in the Doctrine and Covenants. In section 76, for example, we are assured that those who inherit the celestial kingdom will minister to those of the lower kingdoms. Joseph Smith said of those who inherit the telestial kingdom: "These are they who receive not of his fulness in the eternal world, but of the Holy Spirit through the ministration of the terrestrial; and the terrestrial through the ministration of the celestial. And also the telestial receive it of the administering of angels who are appointed to minister for them, or who are appointed to be ministering spirits for them; for they shall be heirs of salvation. And thus we saw, in the heavenly vision, the glory of the telestial, which surpasses all understanding" (D&C 76:86–89).

The Prophet Joseph Smith wrote the whole of section 76 in a poem titled "The Vision," which he sent to William W. Phelps. It acts as a type of commentary on the section. Speaking of the manner of ministering that the inhabitants of higher kingdoms will do for inhabitants of the lower, Joseph used the word "happify." The line reads as follows: "And minist'ring angels, to happify there."[4] What a remarkable verb Joseph used. There are beings who see to the happiness of all the Lord's children regardless of which kingdom of glory their lives merited.

Later in section 76 we are told that even those who receive a telestial glory "shall bow the knee, and every tongue confess to him who sits upon the throne forever and ever; for they shall be judged according to their works, and every man shall receive according to his own works, his own dominion, in the mansions which are prepared; and they shall be servants of the Most High" (D&C 76:110–12).

What a wonderful, breathtaking way to spend eternity: serving the Father, worshipping the Son, and receiving dominion in one of the mansions of the Father. These blessings are extended to all the kingdoms of glory, telestial to celestial. Even in the worst-case scenario, a child who remains apathetic or rebellious and whose life warrants only an inheritance in the telestial kingdom, will eventually accept the cleansing power of the Atonement of Christ, bow the knee, and inherit a kingdom of glory.

Now let us suppose that one of my sons does not live a life worthy of celestial glory. He cannot abide a celestial law, whereas my wife and I remain true to our temple covenants. If, in the eternal worlds, the Lord said, "I need someone to minister to this child, to see to his happiness," who would be the most logical people to reply?

"Lord, let us happify our son! Let us minister to him! We have been true to our covenants. He was bound to us with temple ties. Our love for him has not diminished!"

Would not his grandparents, brothers, and sisters also wish to be part of that happification? I believe they would, and I cannot imagine a God who would deny such a request. We can be calm in the knowledge that all God's children, and therefore all our children, with the exception of those very few who reject the

Savior's infinite gift of mercy and forgiveness, will find eternal contentment and delight in the kingdoms of glory he has prepared. God is in the business of happifying!

## "EVERY HEART WILL CRY, 'MY OWN AGAIN!'"

I am deeply touched by the words of the Scottish author and minister George MacDonald, who in his intuitive comprehension of God as the Father of us all recognized what the Prophet Joseph Smith had taught us through revelation. Speaking of the resurrection, MacDonald wrote: "Every eye shall see the beloved, every heart will cry, 'My own again!—more mine because more himself than ever I beheld him!' . . . What! shall God be the God of the families of the earth, and shall the love that he has thus created towards father and mother, brother and sister, wife and child, go moaning and longing to all eternity; or worse, far worse, die out of our bosoms? Shall God be God, and shall this be the end? Ah, my friends! what will resurrection be to me, how shall I continue to love God as I have learned to love him through you, if I find he cares so little for this human heart of mine, as to take from me the gracious visitings of your faces and forms?"[5]

We can find peace believing that family bonds forged and welded in the house of the Lord and strengthened through righteous commitment or anxious prayer will not be forgotten nor severed in any of the mansions of the Father. The eternal organization of man is family, and in family they shall remain, time without end. The majesty of God's love as evidenced in this vision of the Restoration is matchless in scope. It expands the mind, the heart, and the soul. It bestows a serene tranquility all parents welcome in the fulfillment of their deepest hope—that each of their children may find eternal happiness. The declaration of the Lord is that they shall!

~

## CHAPTER FOURTEEN

The nobleman saith unto him,
Sir, come down ere my child die. Jesus saith unto
him, Go thy way; thy son liveth.
*John 4:49–50*

# The Prayers of a Parent

## IN THE HEART OF A MOTHER

I was twelve when I received my patriarchal blessing. Near its conclusion, the patriarch spoke of my mother and planted in my mind a truth I have come to appreciate more fully the longer I live. It is a truth that at age twelve I could not begin to comprehend, but now, as a parent and grandparent, I feel its penetrating force. I was blessed to walk the straight and narrow path and to seek to fulfill the prayer that would always be in the heart of my mother.

Perhaps, of all the prayers ascending heavenward, that of a parent is keenly heard and considered. One day I should like to hear from my Father in Heaven all the roles my mother's prayers have played in my life. What heavenly help? What influences? What altered circumstances? What forgiveness? What experiences? What people, power, or protection did she pull into my sphere with the magnetic will of her righteous desires? A parent's prayer is a mighty thing.

In full consideration of God's omniscience, his infinite wisdom and his omnipotence, I can only believe that God makes very few plans irrespective of his children's input. Does he not ask us to participate, to engage, in the great plan of happiness? Or does creation proceed machine-like, moving forward like the measured ticking of a clock, in fulfillment of God's all-knowing prophetic gazes? Why does omniscience need asking? Why would not his infinite goodness grant blessings without requests? Why pray at all if the weight of our desire is not added to the scale of God's deliberations? Do not our prayers constitute a major part of our contribution, both to God's work and to our own development?

Indeed, he surely must keep some of his plans unsettled to a degree, intent on waiting to hear the thoughts and desires of his beloved children. If we are one day to share his throne, as promised in scripture, need we not learn, by our own wrestling in the Spirit, how to be admitted to his counsels?

Few requests carry as much feeling as those residing in the heart of a mother or father. It seems to me a rare thing that would take greater priority in his reception of our pleas than those regarding our children—for they are his children also. Our prayers have great power to help others, especially when that is the only help we can give. My love for my child, which sometimes seems powerless to bless that child, moves me to ask assistance of him who is wise, also loves, and can help. We may be assured that God will always do his best for our children. That is inherent in his primary title of "Father." Perhaps both a mortal and a divine parent in combination are necessary in this great laboratory of the soul. Regardless, we read many times in scripture that a parent's pleadings seldom go unheeded.

## "FEAR NOT: BELIEVE ONLY"

A few examples will prove helpful to our understanding of this truth. Jesus in particular was sensitive to the hopes of parents.

"And, behold, there came a man named Jairus, and he was a ruler of the synagogue: and he fell down at Jesus' feet, and besought him that he would come into his house: for he had one only daughter, about twelve years of age, and she lay a dying. . . . While he yet spake, there cometh one from the ruler of the synagogue's house, saying to him, Thy daughter is dead; trouble not the Master. But when Jesus heard it, he answered him, saying, Fear not: believe only, and she shall be made whole" (Luke 8:41–42, 49–50).

We all know the outcome of the story as Jesus "took her by the hand, and called, saying, Maid, arise" (Luke 8:54).

There are times in my own life when I too fear I am troubling the Master about some issue concerning my children, but my heart won't let it rest. These are the moments when I long to hear the comforting words of the Lord whispered through the power of the Spirit: "Fear not! Believe only!" What are we asked to believe in? The answer is evident—the kindness of God, his great goodness, and his willingness to respond to the cry of a mother or father.

There is a sweet beauty in the story of Jairus and his daughter, especially in the Savior's assurance to the father that he should not fear. It portrays the Savior's eagerness to grant the parent's request. We do not get the impression, while reading this story, that Jesus raised Jairus's daughter from her deathbed for any reason related to his broader mission. His compassion was touched. He put everyone out of the room and bade the family "to tell no man what was done" (Luke 8:56). This was pure mercy poured onto the souls of a grieving mother and father.

A like circumstance took place in Nain when the Savior's party came upon a funeral procession. "Now when he came nigh to the gate of the city, behold, there was a dead man carried out, the only son of his mother, and she was a widow: and much people of the city was with her. And when the Lord saw her, he had compassion on her, and said unto her, Weep not. And he came and touched the bier: and they that bare him stood still. And he said, Young man, I say unto thee, Arise. And he that was dead sat up, and began to speak. And he delivered him to his mother" (Luke 7:12–15).

Here was empathy that responded to a mother's grief without request. Her tears were the appeal, and they found a receptive heart. We know that the raising of Lazarus was thought out and planned for in advance, but this act of mercy was spontaneous and shows how the Lord naturally replies to a parent's needs.

While Jesus was with Peter, James, and John on the Mount of Transfiguration, his other disciples could not heal a man's son "which hath a dumb spirit." When he was brought to Jesus, the son fell into a fit, "and wallowed foaming. And he asked his father, How long is it ago since this came unto him? And he said, Of a child. And ofttimes it hath cast him into the fire, and into the waters, to destroy him: but if thou canst do any thing, have compassion on us, and help us. Jesus said unto him, If thou canst believe, all things are possible to him that believeth. And straightway the father of the child cried out, and said with tears, Lord, I believe; help thou mine unbelief" (Mark 9:17, 20–24).

Surely as parents we can all relate to this father. Other sources of help have failed, and we appeal to the Lord's compassion. Can he "do any thing?" We know all things are possible yet fear our own doubts may deny the desired help. We cry out as did this father, "I believe; help thou mine unbelief." Trusting that the Lord always does his best for his children, we put everything in the Lord's hands.

We will not go away without comfort, advice, or assurances of divine assistance.

## WEARY THE LORD

Sometimes the timing of the Lord's answers may allow us to feel despair or test our resolve. During those times we must continue to plead with the Lord, as he taught us in at least two different parables—that of the friend at midnight (see Luke 11:5–13) and the unjust judge (see Luke 18:1–7). In both cases Jesus emphasized the need to continue to ask, to "weary" the Lord, as the widow does in the parable of the unjust judge, knowing we are pleading with a God who delights in answering according to both his mercy and his wisdom.

A case in point is the account of the Canaanite mother who pleaded with Jesus to heal her daughter. After several rebuffs which were more than a test of her resolve, her ardor was only intensified. "Then came she and worshipped him, saying, Lord, help me. But he answered and said, It is not meet to take the children's bread, and cast it to dogs. And she said, Truth, Lord: yet the dogs eat of the crumbs which fall from their master's table. Then Jesus answered and said unto her, O woman, great is thy faith: be it unto thee even as thou wilt. And her daughter was made whole from that very hour" (Matthew 15:21–28).

In this instance, even the seemingly hesitating Christ was persuaded by the intensity of a mother's love, despair, and unwavering need. Joseph Smith once taught that there are times when we need to "come to God, weary him until he blesses you."[1] Because a parent's love is constant, it is not difficult to "weary" God with it.

When the relief of the answered prayer does not come as

quickly as we would wish, we must take comfort in the words the Lord gave to Joseph Smith during the dark troubles of the Missouri persecutions. "Verily I say unto you my friends, fear not, let your hearts be comforted; yea, rejoice evermore, and in everything give thanks; waiting patiently on the Lord, for your prayers have entered into the ears of the Lord of Sabaoth, and are recorded with this seal and testament—the Lord hath sworn and decreed that they shall be granted. Therefore, he giveth this promise unto you, with an immutable covenant that they shall be fulfilled; and all things wherewith you have been afflicted shall work together for your good, and to my name's glory, saith the Lord" (D&C 98:1–3).

## "YE KNOW NOT WHAT YE ASK"

There may be times when the Lord's wisdom must take precedence over our own fervent desires for our children, and, as we discussed in an earlier chapter, say no. Did not the Father answer the Savior's own agonized cry, "Abba, Father, all things are possible unto thee; take away this cup from me" (Mark 14:36), in this manner?

Yet it is difficult to find in the New Testament a time when Jesus declined the pleadings of a parent. Even when we do find such a time, we sense his discomfort in refusing the request. Here is one such example: "Then came to him the mother of Zebedee's children with her sons [James and John], worshipping him, and desiring a certain thing of him. And he said unto her, What wilt thou? She saith unto him, Grant that these my two sons may sit, the one on thy right hand, and the other on the left, in thy kingdom. But Jesus answered and said, Ye know not what ye ask" (Matthew 20:20–22).

When we "know not what we ask," would not our own love for our children welcome the gentle refusal of the Father? Can we not trust that he knows best? The difficulty we face is in perceiving that our present avid desire is just such a case. Here we must be sensitive to the Spirit and ask for discernment concerning our own wishes. This can present the challenge of which Jacob spoke when he considered his own deeply committed hope for the welfare of his people. He was apprehensive that he might be "shaken from [his] firmness in the Spirit, and stumble because of [his] over anxiety for [his people]" (Jacob 4:18). Too much worry can become a barrier which blocks our access to the Holy Ghost's comfort and guidance.

## "GOD HEARS"

It is not only in the life of the Savior that we see sensitivity to a parent's prayers. Stories in the Old Testament also invite us to view the sway of a parent's entreaty. One example is that of Hagar when she and her son, Ishmael, were without water in the wilderness near Beersheba. "And the water was spent in the bottle, and she cast the child under one of the shrubs. And she went, and sat her down over against him a good way off, as it were a bowshot: for she said, Let me not see the death of the child. And she sat over against him, and lift up her voice, and wept."

Hagar had found herself alone in the wilderness once before, while she was pregnant with Ishmael. God heard her in her distress and told her to name the child she was carrying "Ishmael," which means "God hears" (Genesis 16:11). Now, in her present distress, the Lord would fulfill the name of her son. "And *God heard* the voice of the lad; and the angel of God called to Hagar out of heaven, and said unto her, What aileth thee, Hagar? fear not; for *God hath heard* the voice of the lad where he is. . . . And God opened her eyes, and she saw a well of water. . . . And God was with the lad" (Genesis 21:15–17, 19–20; emphasis added).

The beauty of the story strikes deep in our souls as we ponder its relevancy. God hears! The message is simple. When the water is spent in our bottles, sometimes God's hearing consists of his showing us the wells of water we have failed to notice. He reveals to us solutions to relieve the wants of our children or supply their necessities, whether those needs be temporal or spiritual.

Many times as I have cried to the Lord for guidance regarding one of my children, he has responded by showing me the well of water. Ofttimes it was remarkable how obvious the solutions were, but I did not know where to look. Sometimes, as with Jacob, it is because I have hindered the Spirit by my "over anxiety." I find it equally heartening, as we reflect upon the story of Hagar and Ishmael, to read the words, "And God was with the lad." These words have provided immeasurable consolation, especially when my ability or opportunity to bless my children was limited. He not only hears but walks with them.

In the lives of both Elijah and Elisha we witness the faith and prayers of mothers drawing down the blessings of heaven upon their sons. In 1 Kings 17, the son of the widow of Zarephath "fell sick; and his sickness was so sore, that there was no breath left in him" (v. 17). In answer to the mother's anguished words, "Art thou come unto me to call my sin to remembrance, and to slay my son?" Elijah pleaded with the Lord in her behalf (see vv. 18-20). How human is this mother's response—to believe that a negative thing touching her child should arise from her own past or present weakness. "O Lord my God," Elijah cried, "I pray thee, let this child's soul come into him again. And the Lord heard the voice of Elijah; and the soul of the child came into him again, and he revived. And Elijah took the child, and brought him down out of the chamber into the house, and delivered him unto his mother: and Elijah said, See, thy son liveth" (vv. 21-24).

A woman of Shunem, whose wholehearted hospitality and gracious generosity had reached out to Elisha, was rewarded with the birth of a son. "And when the child was grown, it fell on a day, that he went out to his father to the reapers. And he said unto his father, My head, my head. . . . And when he had taken him, and brought him to his mother, he sat on her knees till noon, and then died." With heavy heart the mother went to Elisha for help and "caught him by the feet." Elisha returned with the woman, and exercising all his faith, he "lay upon the child, and put his mouth upon his mouth, and his eyes upon his eyes, and his hands upon his hands: and he stretched himself upon the child; and the flesh of the child waxed warm." At last "the child sneezed seven times, and . . . opened his eyes." Elisha then called for the mother. "And when she was come in unto him, he said, Take up thy son. Then she went in, and fell at his feet, and bowed herself to the ground, and took up her son, and went out" (2 Kings 4:18–20, 27, 34–37).

## THY FATHER HAS PRAYED WITH MUCH FAITH

The Book of Mormon also testifies to the influence of a parent's prayer. The angel who appeared to Alma the Younger as he was going about with the sons of Mosiah seeking to destroy the Church told him: "Alma, who is thy father . . . has prayed with much faith concerning thee that thou mightest be brought to the knowledge of the truth; therefore, for this purpose have I come to convince thee of the power and authority of God, that the prayers of his servants might be answered according to their faith" (Mosiah 27:14).

Perhaps anxious parents wonder why Alma the Younger received the angel and not their child. Are not their prayers as sincere and beseeching as those of Alma's father? In all probability they are.

I suppose one of the very reasons this story was included in the canon was to assure parents that the Lord does respond to their entreaties concerning their children, especially those who have strayed. There are many types of angels, whose shaking of the earth may equally shake a child. Disappointments, tragedies, accidents, new environments or friends, sickness, a death, a birth, a new love, various life changes can all serve the same purpose as Alma's angel.

The important thing to consider is not so much the appearance of the angel in answer to a worried father's pleading but Alma the Younger's reaction to that appearance. He still had to struggle with his past, to be "harrowed up," as he called it (Alma 36:12, 17, 19). Laman and Lemuel also saw an angel, but the change this experience produced in them was only temporary. I think it a fair assumption that had the angel not changed Alma, other efforts would have been made to bring about the necessary amendment and the fulfillment of Alma the Elder's desires for his son.

We certainly can see those additional efforts in the lives of Laman and Lemuel. How many different approaches did the Lord use to try and straighten them out? His arsenal of angels included scriptures, shocks, storms, the Liahona, parental and brotherly rebukes, God's own voice, dreams, hunger, a woman's pleas, Lehi's beseeching dying words, and more.

God keeps sending angels. We don't always know what attempts he has already made, but he does not get discouraged and, therefore, neither should we. Isaiah wrote: "He shall not fail nor be discouraged, till he have set judgment in the earth" (Isaiah 42:4). If the whole world does not dishearten him, our own children will not either.

Let us entreat for our sons and for our daughters. Let us offer to the Eternal Father those sacred hopes that will always lie softly in the hearts of mothers and fathers. These hopes are such a natural part of all our prayers and often represent our most honest and fervent desires. Pleadings of the soul do not go unheeded. They are often the expressions of what God equally yearns for. Perhaps we are never nearer to the heart of our Father in Heaven than during those times when we seek him out in equal love for one of his children. For in those longings in behalf of our sons and daughters we share a kinship with the Lord himself.

## AT THE FOOT OF THE CROSS

Sometimes, in spite of all our prayers and all our devotion, we find ourselves in a position where we must watch a beloved child suffer and we are unable to help. These are, perhaps, the most painful and soul-searching moments a mother or father can face. Of all the poignant scenes in the scriptures involving a parent and child (and there are many), I can think of none that symbolizes or represents these moments quite like that of Mary at the foot of the cross. The scene is presented so simply that we might miss its drama and power if we do not pause a second to visualize it. "Now there stood by the cross of Jesus his mother, and his mother's sister" (John 19:25). Mary witnessed the soldiers gambling for her son's coat, a coat she, in all probability, made herself. "Now the coat was without seam, woven from the top throughout. They said therefore among themselves, Let us not rend it, but cast lots for it, whose it shall be" (John 19:23–24).

The poignancy of Mary's pain is intensified by the knowledge that it had all been prophesied by Simeon on the day Mary and Joseph presented Jesus at the temple when he was a newborn infant. Simeon took Jesus into his arms and thanked God that his eyes had seen his salvation. He then blessed both Mary and Joseph, adding a particularly sobering reflection for Mary. "This child is set for the fall and rising again of many in Israel; and for a sign which shall be spoken against; (*Yea, a sword shall pierce through thy own soul also,*) that the thoughts of many hearts may be revealed" (Luke 2:34–35; emphasis added).

Jesus surely understood his mother's pain and offered to her what comfort he could as he said, "Woman, behold thy son!" Then turning to his beloved disciple, John, he continued, "Behold thy mother!" (John 19:26, 27).

There is much to contemplate in these words. I have wondered about their meaning. To whom did Jesus refer when he asked his mother to behold her son? Was it John, the man who would "from that hour" take Mary "unto his own home" (John 19:27), or the son that hung before her on the cross? I lean to the latter interpretation. When read that way, the emotion of that instant is almost too great to bear. It was Mary's most helpless moment. It was the soul-piercing time of the sword spoken of by Simeon.

At such times in a parent's life, prayer itself may seem insufficient, but it may be all we can do. In a painful time while watching a child face difficult challenges, I found comfort in a story from the book of Acts. Each morning in Jerusalem, "a certain man lame from his mother's womb was carried, whom they laid daily at the gate of the temple which is called Beautiful, to ask alms of them that entered into the temple." In the afternoon, Peter and John walked into the temple precincts at the hour of prayer. As they approached, the lame man looked at them expectantly, hoping for alms. "Peter, fastening his eyes upon him with John, said, Look on us. . . . Then Peter said, Silver and gold have I none; but such as I have give I thee" (Acts 3:2–4, 6).

As I read those words my anxiety and unease calmed. I knew

I could not give my child what was needed, what I so desperately desired to provide. Silver and gold had I none, but that did not mean I had nothing to give. We can only give what we have. There is always love and empathy. Often those are the best of all gifts. The lame man did not receive alms from Peter and John. Rather, Peter "took him by the right hand, and lifted him up" (Acts 3:7).

In a symbolic sense, the ability to take our children by the hand and lift them up with our words, our prayers, our compassion, or our emotional support may bless and help more than we perceive. We need not be fretfully apprehensive or feel we are failing our children when we too sit at the foot of the cross and all we can offer are our tears and the look of love in our eyes.

Above all we must not be swept away by feelings of guilt at the insufficiencies we perceive in our inability to alleviate a child's distress. Jesus' disciples once asked him when they saw a man born blind, "Who did sin, this man, or his parents, that he was born blind? Jesus answered, Neither" (John 9:2–3).

Not all suffering is the direct result of some failure in parent or child. Painful, difficult, and soul-wrenching challenges come into the lives of most of us. Many cannot be prevented, no matter how prescient we may be. These must not become invitations for guilt or self-condemnatory remorse, though we may allow them to become such. It seems to be in the nature of loving parents to feel they could have, or should have, done something to prevent or minimize their children's trials.

## CHAPTER FIFTEEN

We will receive them into our bosom, and they shall
see us; and we will fall upon their necks, and they
shall fall upon our necks, and we will kiss each
other; and there shall be mine abode.
*Moses 7:63–64*

# Building Long-Term Relationships

## THE HOLY TERROR OF THE PRIMARY

As a child, I frequently misbehaved in both school and Primary. My teachers gave me the nickname "Holy Terror of the Primary." I am sure I deserved it. I was not malicious in my disobedience, just too full of boyishness to sit still and listen without interrupting the teacher or talking to my neighbor. I have to admit I was a bundle of mischief waiting for a time and place to break out.

A number of teachers tried various methods to get me to behave. One such was Brother K. He was a former Marine and would brook no nonsense in class. The first time I piped up out of order, he looked me straight in the face and said, "Mike, I understand that you misbehave in class. If you open your mouth or move without permission, I shall bring you to the front of the class and paddle your bare bottom until it is rosy red. Do we understand one another?"

I was as good as gold, but it was sheer terror that motivated me. Sometimes fear of punishment is used to train a child. The Lord uses it as manifested in scripture, and most parents use it; however, it is not very effective over the long term. No truly conscientious parent wishes his child to obey out of fear. Neither does the Lord.

Shortly after Brother K was released Sister M was called to teach our class. She was a frail old widow, and I knew she would not paddle me even if she was tempted to. So I began to misbehave again. After a few weeks she brought into the class a large brown paper bag. She opened it and let the aroma of homemade donuts escape into the room. "Kids," she said, "I know it is very hard to sit still and listen to the lesson. But it is very important for you to learn these scripture stories, so if you will sit still and listen, I will bring you a treat each week."

Again I was as good as gold, but it was the taste of sugar that motivated my actions. Sometimes the promise of a reward is used to train a child. The Lord also uses this. He promises us "the big donut in the sky," as a good friend once said. Yet most parents aren't overly pleased to know that a child is obedient only because he or she expects a reward. Using rewards too, over time, becomes less and less successful.

With the release of Sister M and the assigning of Brother C, my behavior returned to old patterns. After several weeks, Brother C had had enough. He stopped in the middle of the lesson, turned his back on the class, leaned his head on the board, and began to cry. Dead silence reigned.

We began to point fingers at each other, assigning blame. Soon, he turned around and faced the class. "Kids," he said, "it's not your fault. It's mine. I'm just not a good enough teacher to keep you interested. It is so important for you to learn the gospel, and I'm not good enough to teach it to you. You deserve the best, someone who can teach you better. I'm going to go to the bishop and ask to be released so you can have a teacher you will like."

I was stunned. Guilt swept over me, and my own eyes began to fill with tears. We pleaded with him to stay. We promised him we would be good and listen to what he wanted to teach us. He finally agreed and went on with the lesson.

I was good as gold, but it was guilt, pity, and a stinging conscience that motivated my obedience. Parents also use this tactic with their children. I hated it when my mother told me I had disappointed her. I preferred the punishment or reward approach. As a parent, I do not wish my child to be obedient out of a sense of shame or guilt. Those tactics can be effective, but too much guilt too often maims the spirit of a child.

How, then, can we inspire goodness for its own sake, one that arises from children themselves? How does a parent maintain influence in a child's life in a positive way that has staying power long past childhood? I believe the answer lies in a letter Joseph Smith wrote from Liberty Jail and is now found in Doctrine and Covenants 121–23.

## "THE PRINCIPLES OF RIGHTEOUSNESS"

One of the most remarkable revelations we have received from Joseph Smith as it pertains to raising children begins with a question. "There are many called, but few are chosen. And why are they not chosen?" (D&C 121:34). Thus begins Joseph Smith's counsel on eternal, lasting, priesthood leadership. If we consider that a man's family constitutes the most eternal and critical of all possible priesthood callings this section becomes deeply relevant to our discussion of parenting. Let us examine it as both fathers and mothers and apply it solely to our roles as parents.

The reason Joseph gives for few being chosen is their inability to learn one lesson. The Lord is making things simple for us as mothers and fathers. "Please! Learn one lesson!" he says. If we do, we will find our relationships with our children on a solid footing where the threat of punishment, the offering of reward, or the stimulus of guilt becomes unnecessary. The Lord indicates this is a hard lesson to learn, and few seem able to master it. Nonetheless, we must become skilled at this, one of the most conspicuously necessary instructions the Lord has given us in mortality.

What is that lesson? *We must rule, or govern, or preside, or guide our children within the boundaries of the principles of righteousness.* That is the imperative key. Eternal families must be maintained by eternal principles and laws. The "powers of heaven cannot be controlled nor handled only upon the principles of righteousness" (D&C 121:36). We are attempting to forge unending ties here. When we use the principles of righteousness, we have the blessings and assistance of heaven to sanction our efforts. If we try to influence or control our children in any other way, we are bound to fail in the long term. Only one method has the Lord's approval. All other means eventually grieve the Spirit and the heavenly mandate "is withdrawn." When that happens one word expresses the remaining influence—"Amen!" (v. 37). If our influence is not lost completely, it is deeply damaged. "Ere [the parent] is aware," the Lord cautions, "he is left unto himself" (v. 38). A parent may not even notice he is trying to do a very difficult job, in the best of situations and with the best of children, essentially on his own.

Because raising children with the principles of righteousness does not come naturally to us, the Lord reveals a truth about most of us, even in our positions as parents, as a warning. "We have learned by sad experience that it is the nature and disposition of almost all men, as soon as they get a little authority, as they suppose, they will immediately begin to exercise unrighteous dominion. Hence many are called, but few are chosen" (D&C 121:39–40). As a parent, I have a "little authority" over my children, as I "suppose." Ultimately, they are the children of their Father in Heaven. I often remind myself of that fact and that his fathering method incorporates the principles of righteousness.

What are these "principles of righteousness" that hold the key to so much of our future joy and rejoicing in our posterity? Joseph Smith enumerates them with an emphatic beginning that suggests a child's love, trust, respect, reverence, and obedience can only be "maintained" by these principles. "No power or influence can or ought to be maintained by virtue [of my position as parent], *only* by persuasion, by long-suffering, by gentleness and meekness, and by love unfeigned; by kindness, and pure knowledge, which shall greatly enlarge the soul without hypocrisy, and without guile" (D&C 121:41–42; emphasis added).

## PERSUASION

The first principle on the list is a compelling one—that of persuasion. Straightforward commands are always easier, but persuasion is always more effective. When I dictate my will to my child, I do not even need to know in my own mind why I want some particular thing or action. Command is therefore often a mentally lazy way of maintaining control. My will is my will, but with persuasion I must know within myself why I believe the desired behavior, counsel, or decision is correct. Not only must I have compelling reasons known to me but I must also be able to convince another that those reasons represent the best possible solution or direction. Persuasion takes tact, diplomacy, negotiation, respectful compromise. It tends to more peaceful resolutions of disagreements or personality differences.

One of the most compelling examples of a great man using persuasion instead of command is the Apostle Paul as he counseled with the Saints in Corinth. Indeed, Joseph Smith patterned his direction about the principles of righteousness from the writings of Paul (see 2 Corinthians 6:6). Paul often referred to his converts as his children, so the transfer to parental skill is not hard to realize.

The Saints wanted to eat meat offered in pagan festivals to the Greek and Roman gods. They knew these gods were not real, and a piece of meat was just a piece of meat—so why should they not participate in the festive celebrations of their cities with their neighbors? Paul goes through three full chapters (1 Corinthians 8–10) giving reason after reason why this was not a good idea. The interesting thing about this situation is that it had come up before at the Council of Jerusalem, as related in Acts 15. There it was specifically decided by the Twelve Apostles and sent out in an official letter to all the Saints that they were not to eat meat offered to idols. Now, Paul could very easily have saved himself a lot of time and labor by simply telling the Saints, "The Brethren say no!" But he did not use this tactic. He appealed to their better natures and reason, using persuasion and the best thinking he could muster. He was a remarkable leader.

## LONG-SUFFERING

If a parent is going to use persuasion, there will be times that the second principle will be necessary, that of long-suffering. A quick look in a thesaurus tells us that a long-suffering person is patient, forgiving, tolerant, accommodating, and selfless. It can be a challenge sometimes with a child of any age to refrain from becoming a little irritated. In our dealings with our children, the quick retort or silencing command stops the immediate problem, but no teaching or healing has been accomplished. Like scratching an insect bite, it feels good momentarily, but the itch comes back even more fiercely than before. Long-suffering is the lotion that soothes that irritation.

Occasionally we imagine a little frustration in the Savior as he tried to teach his disciples the truths he came to offer. They misunderstood his words, failed to grasp the figurative meaning of a metaphor, or quarreled over who was greatest. When we look at these moments we see him carefully correcting their misconceptions with patient long-suffering. He never turned away or became discouraged with their limits. He worked with the material at hand and raised them to meet his higher expectations. Surely this is one of the reasons people flocked to hear him.

## GENTLENESS

Gentleness is a quality often more readily demonstrated by mothers than fathers. Fathers have to work on this trait more conscientiously, but it pays big dividends. Gentleness is often portrayed in the tone of one's voice, in a touch, in the softness of a look. It recognizes that human beings, despite defensive walls, bluster, or independence, are really very fragile things, especially young children. The gentle parent controls the atmosphere, maintains calm, handles issues quietly and mildly, and is sensitive to the tender feelings of the child.

Little children in particular engender this mildness. Dostoevsky wrote: "Love children especially, for they too are sinless like the angels; they live to soften and purify our hearts, and as it were guide us."[1] Gentleness causes us to weigh our words carefully, considering the effect they might have on another. Gentleness is not confrontational or argumentative, as Paul cautioned Timothy: "The servant of the Lord must not strive; but be gentle unto all men" (2 Timothy 2:24). Gentleness is a feminine-leaning quality that tempers male aggressiveness, as Paul's counsel to Titus indicates: "Be no brawlers, but gentle" (Titus 3:2). The gentle parent "is not easily provoked" (1 Corinthians 13:5). Gentleness is not an easy quality to acquire, for children can sometimes be more than frustrating, but its blessings are usually immediate as well as long-lasting.

## MEEKNESS

Meekness goes hand in hand with a gentle nature. Humility and submissiveness are attached to it. Yet meekness suggests a self-imposed control, not a mandated one. Meekness is power under self-dominion. Perhaps the most enduring portrait of meekness was displayed when Pilate presented the scourged Savior before the people and cried, "Behold the man!"; "Behold your King!" (John 19:5, 14). The mocked Christ was dressed in a purple robe and crowned with thorns. He had been humiliated and scorned, yet he stood there in silent majesty. Here was absolute power, in total command of himself.

Meekness prays, "Father, forgive them; for they know not what they do" (Luke 23:34). Meekness does not assert its own will, is not vindictive, nor is overly concerned about its own dignity. Jesus' triumphal entry into Jerusalem on the back of a donkey fulfilled the prophecy, "Behold, thy King cometh unto thee, meek, and sitting upon an ass" (Matthew 21:5).

Moses was described as "very meek, above all the men which

were upon the face of the earth" (Numbers 12:3). This particular description of him was given at a time when he was severely criticized by his brother, Aaron, and sister, Miriam. The Lord took his part, for it appears from the account that he made no effort to defend himself. A little child represents the perfect understanding of the meekness a parent should aim for. Did not King Benjamin tell his people they must become "as a child, submissive, meek"? (Mosiah 3:19).

## UNFEIGNED LOVE

Unfeigned love has no private agenda but seeks the welfare of the beloved. It is not manipulative or self-seeking. There is no pretense, no deception, no outward facade hiding personal motives, no posturing or affectation. Unfeigned love is charity, pure and simple. In that great masterpiece of Christian literature, it "seeketh not her own" but "beareth all things" (1 Corinthians 13:5, 7).

Unfeigned love does not engage in emotional blackmail. It does not say, "If you loved me, you would _____." It is the love of Ruth and Naomi, totally devoted to the interests and happiness of each other to the point of sacrifice. It is Jonathan's love for David, preferring him even to self-negation, a love David celebrated when he mourned Jonathan's death by saying, "Thy love to me was wonderful, passing the love of women" (2 Samuel 1:26). Solomon relied on unfeigned love when, presented with the conflicting claims of two mothers, he commanded that the disputed infant be cut in two, knowing the true mother would reveal herself.

## KINDNESS

Kindness is most often demonstrated in action. It is empathetic, compassionate, thoughtful, and manifests these feelings by actions. It takes into consideration the weaknesses of others and adapts accordingly. It is not unduly demanding. It is polite in its demeanor, good-mannered—like Boaz's treatment of Ruth while she gleaned in his fields, speaking softly to her, providing water and food and instructing his reapers to "let her glean even among the sheaves . . . and let fall also some of the handfuls of purpose for her, and leave them" (Ruth 2:15-16).

There is a certain grace in kindness, a free bestowing of gifts. It is gracious in its benevolence, grateful for the opportunity to serve. It notices and responds to small needs and service and is usually not manifested in spectacular displays or dramatic benefits. The Old Testament couples this principle with "loving," coining the word "lovingkindness," for love is its motivating force. Nephi indicates it was the Savior's "loving kindness" that enabled him to suffer the pains of the Atonement (1 Nephi 19:9). The Savior's washing of the Apostles' feet demonstrates there is no act too undignified to be encompassed within the realm of kindness (see John 13:1-17). The parable of the sheep and the goats offers the broadest parameters for acts of kindness that are pleasing to the Lord (see Matthew 25:31-46).

## PURE KNOWLEDGE

Pure knowledge comes from the Holy Spirit. It is untainted by human or worldly motives. Parental decisions seek the confirmation and approval of the Spirit. We should "first [obtain our] errand from the Lord" before acting (Jacob 1:17). It is self-discerning, not overzealous—balanced. It brings fervency of purpose without being obsessive or fanatical. It comes after reflection, pondering, searching thought, and prayer. In the same letter from Liberty Jail that contains the great truths we are examining, Joseph Smith wrote the following passage that tells us how to obtain "pure knowledge" that we might "lead [our children] unto salvation":

"A fanciful and flowery and heated imagination beware of; because the things of God are of deep import; and time, and experience, and careful and ponderous and solemn thoughts can only find them out. Thy mind, O man! if thou wilt lead a soul unto salvation, must stretch as high as the utmost heavens, and search into and contemplate the darkest abyss, and the broad expanse of eternity—thou must commune with God."[2]

A love of truth and an aversion to self-deception invite pure knowledge. Pure knowledge suggests application, the idea of creating wisdom from truth so it can be lived. All parents will seek it, for its possession provides a trio for raising a child—the father, the mother, and the Holy Spirit.

## ENLARGE THE SOUL

Doctrine and Covenants 121 speaks of enlarging the soul. In one sense this is what mothers and fathers are commissioned to do with their children, but that is unlikely to take place to the degree desired without the expansion of the parent's own soul. When he compared the word to a seed, Alma the Younger used this expression: "It must needs be that this is a good seed, or that the word is good, for it beginneth to enlarge my soul" (Alma 32:28). This imagery suggests that an enlarged soul is the result of placing the word in the heart and then "nourish[ing] it with great care, that it may get root" (Alma 32:37).

That is one of the great duties of a parent. I cannot plant the seed or nourish it in my child's heart if it is not first flourishing in my own. We learn here one of the results of seeking pure

137

knowledge. It is translated into behavior, into a greater capacity for all of the qualities listed in Doctrine and Covenants 121.

## WITHOUT HYPOCRISY—WITHOUT GUILE

All of the qualities we have discussed must be nurtured and manifested "without hypocrisy, and without guile" (D&C 121:42). We must not expect of our children what we do not demand of ourselves. Sincerity must be supreme. There can be no double standards. If entertainment is not suitable for the child, it should not be suitable for the adult. This principle extends to other activities and attitudes in kind.

My grandmother was a lovely woman, raised in the Church and faithful to it all her days. She became deaf at an early age and became so self-conscious about the large hearing aid she needed that she attended Church meetings only irregularly but encouraged her children to go without her. A number of them are no longer in the Church. I have always been impressed with her last counsel as contained in her life history. She hoped that her descendants would "take their children to church—not send them." It is more important that a parent lead the way than point the way.

To be without guile is to emulate one of the most endearing qualities of childhood itself. Guile brings with it a certain cunning slyness, a clever trickiness, an insincerity that can leave a child uncertain as to the parent's true intentions. It destroys trust. We must not be deceptive or deal in duplicity but be honest and open. Being without guile says to our children, "I have nothing to hide from you. You may know my inner thoughts, motives, and hopes for you." To be without guile means we don't pretend to be doing something for our child's benefit which is really for our own. Our intentions must be so clear that they cannot be misinterpreted. The child's welfare is paramount, and neither the parent nor the child should doubt that truth.

## "STRONGER THAN THE CORDS OF DEATH"

The next principle taught by Joseph Smith deals with those occasional moments when reproof or correction is necessary. This part of Doctrine and Covenants 121 was examined earlier. I would only highlight the need to increase our love afterwards, "that [the child] may know that thy faithfulness is stronger than the cords of death" (v. 44). Faithfulness to our children, a faith that is stronger than death, is also one of the principles of righteousness. When alienation occurs, when compromise cannot be found, when bitter disappointments are experienced, both child and parent know none of these things can break the bond between them. Even though he had "wasted his substance with riotous living," the prodigal son knew where to turn when "no man gave unto him" (Luke 15:13, 16).

I am impressed with a story from China written by a Taoist philosopher named Chuang Tzu who lived in the fourth century before Christ. "Have you not heard of the man of Chia who ran away? Lin Hui threw aside his jade emblem [a suggestion of great wealth, but also of authority] worth a thousand pieces of gold, tied his son to his back and hurried away. People asked, 'Was it because the boy was worth more? Surely a child isn't that valuable. Was it because of all the effort required to carry the jade? But surely a child is even more trouble. So why throw away the jade emblem worth a thousand pieces of gold and rush off with the young child on your back?' Lin Hui told them, 'It was greed that brought me and the jade emblem together, but it was Heaven that linked my son and me together.' When the ties between people are based upon profit, then when troubles come, people part easily. When people are brought together by Heaven, then when troubles come, they hold together."[3]

That hold must be "stronger than the cords of death."

The Lord revealed to Hosea how deeply committed he was to his people, even though "my people are bent to backsliding from me" (Hosea 11:7). "When Israel was a child, then I loved him. . . . I drew them with cords of a man, with bands of love" (Hosea 11:1, 4).

## "CHARITY TOWARDS ALL MEN"

Two more principles are implied in Joseph's letter from Liberty Jail. The first is about our behavior towards those outside our family circle. "Let thy bowels also be full of charity towards all men, and to the household of faith" (D&C 121:45). This is a difficult principle to balance. It is natural to prefer our own above any others, and that is right and proper. But we do have responsibilities towards those outside the sacred circle of family. If we are not careful, in our ardent desires for our own, we may be unjust to others. We may unintentionally instill a degree of selfishness in a child. Charity towards all must tip the scale to an equality measured by fairness. Obligations are owed to our fellow Church members and to the broader society, and these must be taken into consideration. Thus our child also learns to think of others and to sometimes place their needs above his own.

## UNCEASING VIRTUE

The last principle deals with the mind of the mother or father. "Let virtue garnish thy thoughts unceasingly" (D&C 121:45). There is a natural link between this principle of righteousness and that of pure knowledge. We need to concentrate on making our mind a fit and proper place for the Spirit to lodge so that pure knowledge may flow into it and directions concerning our children can be received. The word *virtue* comes from root words that denote the strength which arises from purity. Children draw upon that strength and find comfort in it.

The Prophet Joseph Smith tells us the natural consequence of a virtuous mind: "Then shall thy confidence wax strong in the presence of God" (D&C 121:45). Virtue also exudes a confidence in the presence of sons and daughters. Confidence inspires confidence, just as doubt engenders despair. A child feels the safe environment created by the virtues and convictions of the parent. Here he or she can flourish. The atmosphere created by an assured parent allows children to be free to find their own poise and self-reliance, to believe in themselves and their ability to contribute to their world.

In the *Lectures on Faith*, Joseph Smith indicates that one of the three main pillars upon which faith rests is "an actual knowledge that the course of life which he is pursuing is according to [God's] will."[4] A mind garnished by virtue creates this knowledge and thereby engenders the confidence spoken of in Doctrine and Covenants 121. This in turn leads to greater faith. The child can then follow the parent's lead, also confident that the direction pursued is pleasing to the Lord.

It is difficult to follow the leadership of one who does not have this level of confidence. We want to know that those we follow know where they are going, that they are not hindered by doubt or confusion. Confidence is an essential quality of a mother or father. Unceasing virtue generates it and expands it. Thus, living a virtuous life, even to the extent of our thoughts, is the best way to strengthen belief, to come to an assurance that the gospel is true and good, and to instill it in the soul of a child.

## "WITHOUT COMPULSORY MEANS"

Doctrine and Covenants 121 ends with a beautiful promise, especially compelling when applied to a family. If we as fathers and mothers can maintain our influence in our children's lives by drawing upon the strength of the principles of righteousness, then "the Holy Ghost shall be thy constant companion, and thy scepter an unchanging scepter of righteousness and truth; and thy dominion shall be an everlasting dominion, and without compulsory means it shall flow unto thee forever and ever" (v. 46).

The dominion we are trying to establish is that of our eternal family. A scepter is held by the monarch of a kingdom, symbolizing his or her authority to rule. By virtue of acquiring the principles of righteousness, the scepter and the dominion are unchanging and eternal. We have passed the apprenticeship! We have mastered the test of godliness! But the most marvelous aspect of this closing promise is the willingness of children to remain ever after in the parent's sphere of influence. Within the circle circumscribed by the principles of righteousness and without any exterior compulsion or domination, love, reverence, honor, respect, esteem, deference, desire, obedience, unity, and fondness will flow unto the parent forever and ever.

## CHAPTER SIXTEEN

What mean ye, that ye use this proverb . . . saying,
The fathers have eaten sour grapes, and the
children's teeth are set on edge?
*Ezekiel 18:2*

# Looking to the Future

## "YE SHALL REMEMBER YOUR CHILDREN"

Pondering the consequences of our actions on our children, even if they are not yet born, can be one of the noblest curbs on our own sometimes foolish desires, or one of the finest inspirations for choosing wisely our course of life. This one thing alone will make us better parents and better people. If there is a single outstanding truth the scriptures teach parents it is to consider carefully how their choices will transfer to the rising generations. Parents, or those who one day will be such, may set a standard of behavior for good or ill that may endure through generations stretching down centuries.

We never choose only for ourselves. The idea that "I am only hurting myself. It is my life and I can live it as I please!" is a lie hatched in hell by Lucifer to blind us to responsibilities we will always have toward others. The costs of our choices, no matter what we may say, injure or bless those closest to us, certainly including our children. One need only read of the damaging effects to Michal, daughter of Saul and wife of David, of her father's unjustifiable obsession with destroying David. How disastrous and tragic parents' follies can be for their children! (see 1 Samuel 18, 19, 25; 2 Samuel 3, 6).

No clearer example of this truth can be shown than that of Laman and Lemuel. How many centuries of animosity, hatred, and war did these two foolish, ambitious fathers bequeath to their descendants? Lehi could foresee the coming tragedy and blessed his grandchildren accordingly. Lehi "called the children of Laman . . . and said unto them. . . . I cannot go down to my grave save I should leave a blessing upon you; for behold, I know that if ye are brought up in the way ye should go ye will not depart from it. Wherefore, if ye are cursed, behold, I leave my blessing upon you, that the cursing may be taken from you and answered upon the heads of your parents" (2 Nephi 4:3, 5–6). The same blessing was then given to the children of Lemuel.

During the crisis Jacob faced with the fathers of his generation, he too taught the principle so clearly seen in Lehi's last blessings. "Wherefore, ye shall remember your children, how that ye have grieved their hearts because of the example that ye have set before them; and also, remember that ye may, because of your filthiness, bring your children unto destruction. . . . O my brethren, hearken unto my words; arouse the faculties of your souls; shake yourselves that ye may awake from the slumber of death" (Jacob 3:10–11). Jacob knew that even though the fathers were "beginning to labor in sin" (Jacob 2:5), there was still innate goodness within them. He appealed to those faculties of the soul that they had allowed to "slumber," particularly those parental feelings that can be such a motivation for righteousness. Jacob felt the most effective thing to cause that awakening was the thought of how their actions would set the direction of their children's destiny.

## THE INGRAINED POWER OF TRADITION

One of the saddest things we see every day in this weary world is the transmission of hate and anger to succeeding generations until it reaches the ingrained power of a tradition. One need look only to the Middle East, or Central Africa, or a dozen other places in the world where young children are raised on the prejudices of their elders. Many of these problems span multiple centuries.

Zeniff told the Nephites as they prepared to defend themselves against a coming attack from the Lamanites, "They have taught their children that they should hate them, and that they should murder them, and that they should rob and plunder them, and do all they could to destroy them; therefore they have an eternal hatred towards the children of Nephi" (Mosiah 10:17). In 4 Nephi a similar phenomenon is seen as the once-united people divide into factions. "They did willfully rebel against the gospel of Christ; and they did teach their children that they should not believe. . . . It was because of the wickedness and abomination of their fathers, even as it was in the beginning. And they were taught to hate the children of God" (4 Nephi 1:38–39).

Jesus taught with a powerful illustration how serious it is to offend a child. "But whoso shall offend one of these little ones which believe in me, it were better for him that a millstone were hanged about his neck, and that he were drowned in the depth of the sea. . . . It must needs be that offences come; but woe to that man by whom the offence cometh" (Matthew 18:6–7). We usually think of this verse in terms of physically hurting a child, but is it not equally serious to instill such evil emotions as hate or prejudice into the natural loveliness of a child's innocence?

## "THEIR YOUNG ONES SHALL LIE DOWN TOGETHER"

Of all the wonderful, positive, edifying, constructive, and praise-worthy things a parent can teach a child, what a thoughtless travesty it is that hate and bigotry are so often passed on and with a deliberateness that, if directed to good things, could have produced such contrasting results. One of the loveliest prophecies of Isaiah deals with the lamb and the wolf, the leopard and the kid, the calf and the young lion. These, we are told, will all lie down together in peace. This is not a prophecy about animals, however. If we read it literally we may miss a profoundly beautiful message of hope. It speaks of the relations of men, of nations, and the far too common tendency of humankind to resort to the law of the jungle, the law of the predator, in their relationships. It is a prophecy that speaks of the end of wars and conflicts and the hatreds, distrusts, and angers which bring them on.

Part of that prophecy is addressed to the peace one generation will pass down to the next. Isaiah writes: "And the cow and the bear shall feed; their young ones shall lie down together" (Isaiah 11:7). When the cub sees that the bear is at peace with the cow, it will cease to prey upon it. When the calf sees the cow trusting the bear, it will cease to fear it. The example of the parent will transfer to the child. Just as it takes only one generation to start hate, it takes but one to end it. That is the immense tragedy of world conflict. As Jesus said, "This is the condemnation, that light is come into the world, and men loved darkness rather than light" (John 3:19). When the animosity of the parents disappears, the children will learn harmony, concord, and serenity. Then "they shall not hurt nor destroy in all my holy mountain" (Isaiah 11:9).

Speaking in a similar vein in the Doctrine and Covenants, the Lord stresses the blessing that will be granted if we can avoid conflict, even to the point of turning the cheek not once but a second, a third, and a fourth time. "Thou shalt be rewarded for thy righteousness; and also thy children and thy children's children unto the third and fourth generation" (D&C 98:30).

We must be so very wise as parents when we consider the effects upon our children of what we teach. We will not transmit hostilities and grievances to the innocent, where destructive results play out generation upon generation. We should not do this even to the extent of something as seemingly innocent as sporting rivalries. How can intense dislike or animosity ever be healthy for a child or an adult to foster?

The opposite is always possible. Parents can establish traditions of tolerance, kindness, and brotherly love. When God chose Abraham to be the father of the faithful, the founding progenitor of a posterity that would bless the world with so much truth and so much goodness, one of his main considerations was the constructive effect Abraham would have on the future. "And the Lord said, Shall I hide from Abraham that thing which I do; seeing that Abraham shall surely become a great and mighty nation, and all the nations of the earth shall be blessed in him? For I know him, that he will command his children and his household after him, and they shall keep the way of the Lord, to do justice and judgment" (Genesis 18:17–19).

## THE TEMPLE OF A CHILD'S SOUL

In his first epistle to the Corinthians, Paul created a powerful metaphor that may be helpful for parents as they consider what moral or spiritual legacies they are bequeathing to their posterity. Paul was concerned that various teachers who had arrived in Corinth were teaching doctrines and behavior not consistent with truth. The people themselves were dividing into groups, each championing a different teacher or approach to the gospel. With those issues in mind, Paul compared the Church to a temple and called himself a "masterbuilder" (1 Corinthians 3:10), who had laid a solid foundation. He warned the Saints to be careful what they added to that temple:

"Now if any man build upon this foundation gold, silver, precious stones, wood, hay, stubble; every man's work shall be made manifest: for the day shall declare it, because it shall be revealed by fire; and the fire shall try every man's work of what sort it is. If any man's work abide which he hath built thereupon, he shall receive a reward. If any man's work shall be burned, he shall suffer loss. . . . Know ye not that ye are the temple of God, and that the Spirit of God dwelleth in you? If any man defile the temple of God, him shall God destroy; for the temple of God is holy, which temple ye are" (1 Corinthians 3:12–17).

Here Paul was speaking of the teachings, doctrines, ideas, habits, ethics, or morals various individuals may place in the minds of the Saints. Some of those teachings could be compared to gold or precious gems and would be appropriate to the overall beauty of the temple. Some would be wood or hay or stubble and would not fit the symmetry, ambiance, or structural integrity of the building. The fiery trials of life would test the endurance, the quality, the strength of what each individual added or allowed to be added.

The souls of our children are like Paul's temple. We need only look at pictures of the perfection of loveliness and proportion seen in the Greek temples of Paul's time or our modern Latter-day Saint temples to grasp the idea of the apostle's metaphor. The great truths of eternity are like the marble pillars and carved pediments Paul knew or the granite solidity and heaven-reaching spires of our own temples. How unseemly it would be to add barn wood or bales of hay or straw to the architectural dignity of marble and granite! Each thing we teach our children adds something to the temple of his or her soul. We must constantly ask ourselves if it fits the beauty God himself, as the ultimate master builder, placed as the foundation. Am I adding enduring gold or worthless stubble? Only that which is good and true and beautiful can withstand the fires of life. Time will determine the quality of our workmanship. Let us build thereon only those things that will abide, for then we will reap the reward of joy and rejoicing in our posterity. Let us place nothing in the temple of our children's hearts and minds that God will need to purge before he places them in his eternal city.

⌒

## CHAPTER SEVENTEEN

And Jesus called a little child unto him, and set him
in the midst of them, and said, . . . I say unto you,
That in heaven their angels do always behold the
face of my Father which is in heaven.
*Matthew 18:2–3, 10*

# "Behold Your Little Ones"

## "FATHER, I AM TROUBLED"

Perhaps a fitting end to a study of what the scriptures teach about raising children would be the Savior's actions with the little children as recorded in 3 Nephi. This is especially appropriate because in the Savior's visit we get a sense of how deeply concerned about children the Father and the Son are. Toward the end of his first day's visit, Jesus "commanded that their little children should be brought. So they brought their little children and set them down upon the ground round about him, and Jesus stood in the midst." The Lord asked the people to kneel and pray with him in behalf of their children. Immediately prior to that united prayer, as he was kneeling on the ground, "Jesus groaned within himself, and said: Father, I am troubled because of the wickedness of the people of the house of Israel" (3 Nephi 17:11–14).

I have pondered that groan many times and wondered what was

behind it. *Groaned* is the same word used in the Gospel of John at the raising of Lazarus when he saw the distress of Mary and Martha. "He groaned in the spirit, and was troubled" (John 11:33). At that time he was profoundly touched by the weeping and sorrow around him. I think we have a similar moment in the description of Jesus just before he prayed in Gethsemane. Here he is described as being "sore amazed, and . . . very heavy." He then said to Peter, James, and John, "My soul is exceeding sorrowful" (Mark 14:33, 34). Yet with the Nephites and Lamanites all was joy and blessedness.

I believe the Savior was deeply moved by the innocence, the purity and wholesome loveliness, of little children who would have to grow up in a morally contaminated and wicked world. It troubled him to the core of his being. I think he was aware of all the children who were not among those who sat calmly at his feet, those who would not have the promising future those children would have. I sense in that groan a love and a hope that all his Father's children might be raised in happiness, in goodness—cared for by devoted parents, not perfect ones but parents who understood the mighty weight of their responsibility. Yet so many little ones come into spiritually damaging situations.

Then he "prayed unto the Father, and the things which he had prayed cannot be written" (3 Nephi 17:15). Even the intense prayers of Gethsemane were recorded, the great intercessory prayer and his pleading that the cup be removed, but here things were said and seen that were either beyond the capacity of words or were too sacred for the page.

## "ENCIRCLED ABOUT WITH FIRE"

Having emptied his soul, he rose and wept anew, telling them his joy was full. Still not content with his spiritual labors in behalf of the children, "he took their little children, one by one, and blessed them, and prayed unto the Father for them. And when he had done this he wept again" (3 Nephi 17:21–22). We are told that a picture is worth a thousand words. Could any words have depicted more clearly or with greater poignancy the desires of our Savior, and the Father to whom he prayed, towards children? Can we possibly doubt how immeasurably important it is to provide the best of worlds for our own children?

The Savior provided yet another testimony of a child's worth and the need for diligent nourishing of each one. "Behold your little ones," he said. "And as they looked to behold they cast their eyes towards heaven, and they saw the heavens open, and they saw angels descending out of heaven as it were in the midst of fire; and they came down and encircled those little ones about, and they were encircled about with fire; and the angels did minister unto them" (3 Nephi 17:23–24).

Encircled with fire! That is what the God we worship desires to protect his children. Yet his great plan of happiness allows them to be placed in our care, for our instruction and development as well as theirs. In harmony with his wisdom and exalting plan of redemption, he may not continually encircle them with light, with truth, with goodness here. But the Lord's fervent hope is that we will, that we will minister to them as did the angels on that evening in Bountiful as the first day's visit of the Savior drew to a close.

There was one more monumental truth Jesus had yet to teach these parents as they viewed their children. For three days he shared himself and his truths with them. Part of that time was devoted to their children, for we read: "And it came to pass that he did teach and minister unto the children of the multitude of whom hath been spoken, and he did loose their tongues, and *they did speak unto their fathers great and marvelous things, even greater than he had revealed unto the people;* and he loosed their tongues that they could utter. . . . [And] the multitude gathered themselves together, and they both saw and heard these children; yea, even babes did open their mouths and utter marvelous things; and the things which they did utter were forbidden that there should not any man write them" (3 Nephi 26:14, 16; emphasis added).

For whom did the Savior reserve such marvelous teachings? Not the high priests. Not the Relief Society. Not even his chosen Twelve! No, his greatest truths—"even greater than he had revealed unto the people"—were given to "the children of the multitude," who were then allowed to share those precious realities with their parents.

Here was heaven's divine sanction of the sacred teaching within a family. There is a godly humbling there too, for are we not taught that the child best represents the kingdom of heaven? Though I know our children are sent to us so we can teach and shape them for eternity, perhaps the greatest shaping is being done by them for our benefit. For this we can be grateful and add that gratitude to our joy in them. Surely the Savior would say to us all, "Behold, your little ones! Listen to your little ones! Learn from your little ones! They have so much to teach you!"

# Notes

### Introduction

1. Confucius, *Analects*, trans. D. C. Lau (New York: Penguin Books, 1979), I:2.

### Chapter One: The Divine Apprenticeship

1. Brigham Young, *Journal of Discourses*, 26 vols. (London: Latter-day Saints' Book Depot, 1854–86), 3:356.

### Chapter Two: Genesis—First Families, First Lessons

1. LDS Bible Dictionary, s.v. "Manasseh," 728, and "Ephraim," 666.

### Chapter Four: The Lens of a Mother's Soul

1. Joy Webb Rigby, "Living by the Spirit," *Ensign*, August 1984, 15.

### Chapter Five: Stir Up Their Faith to Feel After God

1. Joseph Smith, *Lectures on Faith* (Salt Lake City: Deseret Book, 1985), 2:33–34; emphasis added.
2. Smith, *Lectures on Faith*, 2:56; emphasis added.

3. "Letter to an Unknown Lady" (1866), in *An Expression of Character: The Letters of George MacDonald*, ed. Glen Edward Sadler (Grand Rapids, Mich.: Eerdmans, 1994), 154.

## Chapter Seven: Enlarging the Memory

1. Arthur Henry King, *The Abundance of the Heart* (Salt Lake City: Bookcraft, 1986), 107.
2. *The Works of Mencius*, trans. James Legge (New York: Dover Publications, 1970), 392.
3. *Fern-seed and Elephants*, ed. Walter Hooper (Glasgow, Scotland: Fount Paperbacks, 1977), 35.

## Chapter Eight: Praise and Validation

1. Lucy Mack Smith, *History of Joseph Smith by His Mother* (Salt Lake City: Bookcraft, 1954), 79.

## Chapter Nine: Nurture and Admonition

1. Brigham Young, *Journal of Discourses*, 26 vols. (London: Latter-day Saints' Book Depot, 1854–86), 8:367.

## Chapter Ten: Creating an Enviornment

1. *Mencius*, rev. ed., trans. D. C. Lau (Hong Kong: Chinese University Press, 2003), 63.
2. See ibid., 343.

## Chapter Eleven: Learning to Say No

1. John F. Kennedy, *Profiles in Courage* (New York: Harper and Row, 1955), 50.

## Chapter Twelve: Helping the Struggling and the Wayward

1. Howard W. Hunter, "Parents' Concern for Children," *Ensign*, November 1983, 65.

## Chapter Thirteen: "And Minist'ring Angels, to Happify There"

1. Orson F. Whitney, Conference Report, April 1929, 110.
2. Brigham Young, *Discourses of Brigham Young*, sel. John A. Widtsoe (Salt Lake

City: Deseret Book, 1954), 208. See also Boyd K. Packer, "Our Moral Environment," *Ensign*, May 1992, 66–68.

3. See James E. Faust, "Dear Are the Sheep That Have Wandered," *Ensign*, May 2003, 61–62, 67–68.

4. Lyndon Cook, *Revelations of Joseph Smith* (Provo, Utah: Seventies Mission Bookstore, 1981), 165; "A Vision," *Times and Seasons* 4 (1 February 1843): 82–85.

5. George MacDonald, *Unspoken Sermons* (Charleston, S.C.: BiblioBazaar, 2006), 117–18.

## Chapter Fourteen: The Prayers of a Parent

1. Andrew F. Ehat and Lyndon W. Cook, eds., *Words of Joseph Smith* (Provo, Utah: Brigham Young University Religious Studies Center, 1980), 15.

## Chapter Fifteen: Building Long-Term Relationships

1. Fyodor Dostoevsky, *The Brothers Karamazov*, trans. Constance Garnett (New York: Modern Library, 1996), 357.

2. Joseph Smith, *History of The Church of Jesus Christ of Latter-day Saints*, ed. B. H. Roberts, 7 vols. 2d ed. rev. (Salt Lake City: The Church of Jesus Christ of Latter-day Saints, 1932–51), 3:295.

3. *The Book of Chuang Tzu*, trans. Martin Palmer (New York: Penguin Books, 1996), 171–72.

4. Joseph Smith, *Lectures on Faith* (Salt Lake City: Deseret Book, 1985), 3:5.

# Index